THE RURAL INDUSTRIES
OF ENGLAND & WALES

II
OSIER-GROWING AND BASKETRY
AND SOME RURAL FACTORIES

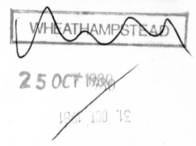

PEAT BED AT MEARE, SOMERSET

THE RURAL INDUSTRIES OF ENGLAND & WALES

A SURVEY MADE ON BEHALF OF THE AGRICULTURAL ECONOMICS RESEARCH INSTITUTE OXFORD

II
OSIER-GROWING AND BASKETRY AND SOME RURAL FACTORIES

By
HELEN E. FITZRANDOLPH
and M. DORIEL HAY

EP Publishing Limited
1977

First published Oxford University Press, 1926

Republished 1977 by
EP Publishing Limited
East Ardsley, Wakefield
West Yorkshire, England

Copyright © 1977 Oxford University Press

ISBN o 7158 1232 7

British Library Cataloguing in Publication Data
FitzRandolph, Helen E
  The rural industries of England & Wales.
  2 : Osier-growing and basketry and some
  rural factories.
  1. England – Rural conditions 2. England –
  Industries – History
  I. Title II. Hay, M Doriel III. Jones, A M
  IV. University of Oxford. Agricultural Economics
  Research Institute
  338'.0942   HC255
  ISBN 0-7158-1232-7

Please address all enquiries to EP Publishing Limited
(address as above)

Printed in Great Britain by
The Scolar Press Limited
Ilkley, West Yorkshire

PREFACE

In any consideration of the development of the country-side the place and function of local industries in rural life must occupy a prominent position. Their importance in the past is obvious, when the village was largely an isolated economic unit ; in view of the part they might still play in maintaining a fuller life for the country dweller, in stemming the flow of population from the rural to the urban centres, and in solving some of the problems of modern industrialism, the need for a study of their present state, of the extent to which the changes in modern, social, and economic conditions demand their supersession, and of the possibility of adapting and developing them to serve these same conditions, becomes increasingly apparent.

It may be that rural industries can continue to supplement agriculture in the complete rural community, by providing subsidiary employment for the part-time land-worker and the small-holder ; by affording the chance of employment in their own homes or villages to the various members of their families ; by providing certain requisites of agricultural industry. It may be possible that in the revolution of economic principles and systems which is now being made by all sorts and conditions of persons, certain human advantages in rural industries may be set against the greater production of goods by the larger industrial units of the towns. In particular, the smaller industrial concern enables a man to see the whole series of connexions between the making and using of an article, and brings his work into direct relation not only with his own life, but with that of the community of which he is a member. There is little or no distinction between producer and consumer and one of the chief causes of present social conflicts is non-existent. The worker in the country 'sees the nature of what he is doing; he is getting products from the land and making use of them by industry. He sees the whole process, and the fact is plain that labour and land are for the sake of himself and others like him who needs the goods. He sees the grain become flour, the wood from the forest become furniture, the hide become leather, and the leather boots, and the wool cloth— all beside him, and all of it a plain process of natural goods made useful by men.' [1] The men of the towns, however, have a genius for organization, and if it be necessary that their business should be arranged on a basis involving less specialization than at present, or so that some of the evil effects of over-specialization were eliminated, they may be able to modify existing systems without seriously affecting their productivity. The only basis upon which rural industries can be firmly established is that of a high standard of technical knowledge and skill, suitable machinery, and commercial organization. On the other hand, the moribund condition of many once-flourishing country trades and crafts may have to be recognized as the price of industrial progress in other centres. The modern tendency towards the centralization of industry and large-scale production; the enormous development of transport facilities which has broken down the barriers between town and country; the danger of these small unorganized enterprises becoming sweated industries serving only to subsidize agricultural wages, all of these things may render undesirable any effort towards the resuscitation of many of these ancient crafts.

With so little knowledge available it became clear that a thorough investigation of the position of rural industries, both economic and social, would be advantageous and, in 1919, at the suggestion of the Development Commissioners, an inquiry into the condition of rural industries in the neighbourhood of Oxford was set on foot by the Agricultural Economics Research Institute, at Oxford. It was rather of the nature of a trial trip, an experimental inquiry to explore the possibilities of a more complete investigation, and

[1] D. H. Macgregor, *The Evolution of Industry*, p. 24.

in the following year arrangements were made with the Development Commissioners and the Ministry of Agriculture for an extension of the survey so as to bring under review the principal rural industries of England and Wales.

The terms of reference of those responsible for the work were to consider—

(1) the existing rural industries and the causes of their establishment in particular localities, such as easy access to local supplies of raw material and labour, and local markets for the finished products ;

(2) the various types of organization in these industries, such as small factories and workrooms or individual pro- duction, organizations for the purchase of raw materials or the sale of finished products. Educational facilities and the possibilities of technical instruction were also to be borne in mind in this connexion ;

(3) the economic and social effects of rural industries, the conditions of labour attendant on them, the connexion between rural industries and agricultural employment, and how far such industries tend to depress or to ameliorate the lot of the agricultural worker ;

(4) the prospects of development of existing industries and of the introduction of new enterprises, or of the resuscitation of former industries now dead or in a state of suspended animation. In this connexion the existence of competition, both urban and foreign, was to be borne in mind, and con- sideration given to the conditions under which rural indus- tries can compete with urban production.

The survey was carried out during three years by a specially appointed group of workers. They surveyed the country, county by county, and the results of their inquiries were embodied in reports dealing with the industries of particular localities. From these interim reports (which are available in manuscript, for consultation, at Oxford) the final reports were compiled, dealing with the various industries separately as they occur throughout the country.

As has already been said, the first district surveyed was that of Oxfordshire, and the investigator in this instance

was Miss K. S. Woods, who was assisted in part of the
work by Miss C. D. Biggs. The results of the survey were
embodied in book form, and published early in 1921.[1] From
1921 to 1922 the work was continued by Miss Woods and
Miss Helen FitzRandolph, and in the summer of 1922 Miss
M. Doriel Hay took Miss Woods's place. The survey of
the Welsh industries required a knowledge of the Welsh
language and was undertaken, apart from the English survey,
by Miss A. M. Jones, in 1922 and 1923. All these investigators worked under the direction of Mr. A. W. Ashby.
A list of the districts surveyed by each is appended.

The investigators must be congratulated upon the results
of their work. Inquiries of this kind are not always too
easily conducted, and call for a measure of enthusiasm and
even of courage in those concerned if the best results are
to be obtained.

It is impossible to name all those who assisted them in
their work, but I should like to make grateful acknowledge-
ment of the friendly reception accorded to them, and of the
readiness with which those engaged in the various industries
investigated gave of their time and knowledge. Without
their cordial co-operation it would have been an impossible
task.

For convenience of publication the reports have been
collected together in four volumes, as follows :

Vol.   I. Timber and Underwood Industries and some
           Village Workshops.
Vol. II. Osier-Growing and Basketry, and Some Rural
           Factories.
Vol. III. Decorative Crafts and Rural Potteries.
Vol. IV. Rural Industries in Wales.

The following report is Vol. II of the series.

C. S. ORWIN.

AGRICULTURAL ECONOMICS
    RESEARCH INSTITUTE,
        OXFORD, *July 1926.*

[1] K. S. Woods, *Rural Industries Round Oxford* (Oxford University Press).

ORDER OF THE SURVEY

Date.	District.	Investigator.
1919–20	Oxfordshire	K. S. Woods and C. D. Biggs
1920–1	Bedfordshire	Helen FitzRandolph
1921	Derbyshire, Leicestershire, and Nottinghamshire	,,
1921–2	Kent, Surrey, and Sussex	,,
,,	Westmorland, Cumberland, and Lancashire	,,
1922	Shropshire, Staffordshire, and Cheshire	K. S. Woods
,,	Herefordshire and Worcestershire	,,
,,	South Western Counties	,,
,,	Durham	Helen FitzRandolph
,,	Northumberland	,,
,,	North Riding of Yorkshire	Helen FitzRandolph and M. Doriel Hay
,,	East and West Ridings of Yorkshire	M. Doriel Hay
,,	Carnarvonshire	A. M. Jones
,,	Denbighshire	,,
,,	Flint	,,
1923	Gloucestershire	Helen FitzRandolph
,,	East Anglia and Essex	,,
,,	Lincolnshire	M. Doriel Hay
,,	Warwickshire	,,
,,	East Midland Counties	,,
,,	Merionethshire and Montgomeryshire	A. M. Jones
,,	Brecon and Radnorshire	,,
,,	Pembrokeshire, Cardiganshire, Carmarthenshire, and Anglesey	,,
,,	Monmouthshire and Glamorganshire	,,

CONTENTS

PART I

OSIER-GROWING AND BASKETRY INDUSTRIES

PART II

FACTORIES IN RURAL DISTRICTS AND OUT-WORK FOR FACTORIES

ILLUSTRATIONS

PART I. OSIER-GROWING AND BASKETRY INDUSTRIES

CHAPTER I

INTRODUCTORY

THE plaiting of willow or other pliant rods, rushes, or grass into baskets is one of the oldest crafts, the origin of textile weaving, and dates from prehistoric times. Although the artist and the skilled craftsman find scope in the making of baskets for the exercise of their powers, and the methods of growing and preparing the rods used have been the subject of long and careful study by experts, yet, in its essential characteristics, this is one of the simplest of crafts, involving only the manipulation of the rods by the hands of the worker.

The first basket-makers, without doubt, cut their rods from the thickets and undergrowth, as gipsies and other primitive basket-makers do at the present day. As the craft developed, the workers would begin to cultivate osiers in order to provide a good supply, and would naturally select those varieties best suited to their needs. Thus the modern cultivation of osiers had its origin, but the careful study of the possibilities of osier growing is a very recent development.

The plaiting of rushes into baskets, mats, and other things is a craft closely allied to osier basket-making, but in England, at least, it is carried on only in a very small way, and has not been so elaborately developed as the other craft. The material used, rushes and sedge, is cut from the rivers and broads, not being cultivated in any way.[1]

The craft of basketry is practised by nearly all primitive peoples ; in the more civilized countries it is found both as a peasant industry and also on a larger, more commercial scale. Baskets have been discovered in the tombs of the Pharaohs, and the wattle huts and boats made by the

---

[1] See Chapter III. Rush, Sedge, and Reed Industries, p. 93.

ancient Britons were a primitive form of basketry, surviving to-day in the wattle hurdle. Herodotus tells of the wattle shields, and arrows made of osiers, used by some of the nations whom Xerxes led against the Greeks. The very origin of the word ' basket ' is lost in the darkness of antiquity. The art of basketry was already old when that of making clay pots was in the early stages of its development, for, before the invention of the potter's wheel, the clay vessels were shaped in a basket-mould, and the imprint of the design of the twisted rods on the wet clay was the origin of the earliest form of decoration on pottery.

The basket-makers themselves supply the needs of many different types of people. Their products are found alike in the potato fields and the orchards, and on the quays of fishing ports, for these men make the rough vessels which receive the fruits of the earth and the harvests of the sea. Turn to the busiest centres of industrial life, and baskets are in use in the Yorkshire woollen mills or the Northamptonshire boot factories. There are also the numerous articles of wicker work, from shopping baskets to arm chairs, which are in daily use in the houses of rich and poor. There is probably no other rural industry of which the output is so varied and in such widespread demand.

Although baskets are so universally made and used, and are of innumerable shapes and kinds, adapted to the various needs, yet it is remarkable that the actual process of making has changed in no important particular throughout the ages, and no satisfactory method has yet been found for the application to it of machinery.

CHAPTER II

OSIER-GROWING AND BASKET-MAKING

I. *The Geographical Distribution of the Osier-growing and Basket-making Industries.*

WILLOWS are known all over the habitable world, but they grow most abundantly in temperate or even cold climates. It is generally considered by authorities that the kind of soil best suited to basket willows is a rich, well-watered, heavy loam, but it has been found that they also do well on dry, sandy ground with a good top soil of about six inches in depth, on poor loamy clay, and even on peaty soils. There are only a few districts in England where osiers [1] are cultivated extensively and scientifically, and they all fall into one or other of these classes as regards soil. In nearly every county, however, willows are grown to some extent, in small plots, generally with very indifferent care, and they are to be found in their wild state all over England. In the osier-growing districts of Nottinghamshire and Leicestershire the soil is a rich loam, in Lancashire it is sandier in quality and suited especially to one particular variety of willow, whilst in Somerset it varies from the rich loam of a river bank to the peaty moss, which, though poor, is still acceptable to the osier.

The willow-growing area of Nottinghamshire and Leicester-shire is the most important of these districts. It is the district in which some of the first experiments were made, by William Scaling of Basford, to improve the quality of willows, though whether he chose the banks of the Trent for his experiments simply because he happened to live there, or whether he lived near the Trent because he con-

---

[1] Strictly speaking, the term ' osier ' applies only to *S. viminalis*, one of the three groups of willows suitable for basketry (the other two being *S. triandra* and *S. purpurea*). The distinctive terminology is often preserved in Nottinghamshire, amongst the most scientific growers ; in Somerset all the finer kinds of rods are loosely called ' osiers ', the coarser kinds being simply termed ' rods '. Amongst basket-makers in general and the less careful growers the terms ' osier ', ' willow ', or ' rod ' are applied indiscriminately or with varying connotations, and therefore they are, of necessity, used in this general way in this report.

sidered it the most suitable district for these experiments, is not known. At any rate, the valley of the Trent and its tributaries is essentially suited to the growth of the basket willow, and the standard of cultivation there is above that of any other district.

Basket-making is carried on in every county of England, and the distribution of the industry in rural districts corresponds to some extent to the chief osier-growing areas, although the existence of some special local demand for baskets accounts for the existence of basket-making workshops in some districts where few osiers are grown. In the notable osier-growing areas, such as the Trent Valley, the Bridgwater district (Somerset), and Mawdesley (Lancs.), where soil and climate particularly favour their cultivation, the basket-making industry has probably arisen in order to make use of the locally grown raw material, but in other areas, such as Cambridgeshire, Worcestershire, and Gloucestershire, some local demand for baskets has given rise to a certain amount of osier cultivation.

The valley of the Trent and its tributaries, the Soar, Derwent, Dove, and Idle, is the most important district in England for both osier-growing and basket-making, not only from the point of view of quantity of output, but also for the quality of the rods and the care given to their cultivation and for the fineness of the basketry work done here. The Trent Valley is low lying and peculiarly liable to floods. It is tidal for some distance above Gainsborough, and until the dykes which now guard the meadows were built, some seventy to eighty years ago, it was the custom of the river to rush in upon the land at every flood tide, that is, about once a fortnight.

Official statistics give the area of land under willows in Nottinghamshire, in 1917, as 750 acres ; in Leicestershire, including the areas at Thurmaston, Loughborough, Barrow-on-Soar, and Castle Donington, there might be another two or three hundred acres ; in Lincolnshire, near Gainsborough and around Grantham, perhaps another 200 acres altogether. The outstanding features of willow-growing in this district are the high standard of cultivation and the large size of the beds. At Castle Donington there are a number of small beds, owned and worked by individual basket-makers, but in most places the beds range from 20 to 50 acres, and at Thurmaston and Grantham there are beds of a hundred acres each.

The following figures, relating to the Trent Valley area,

will show that even in a district where osier-growing is an
important industry, the acreage under osiers is small in
comparison with the acreage of agricultural land. The
figures for gross rentals give some idea of the relative values
of osier beds and agricultural land.

Castle Donington (notable both for osier-growing and for
basket-making).

Agricultural land . . . . . about 2,660 acres
Osier beds . . . . . . about   32 acres
(A proportion of approximately 83 to 1)

These records were incomplete, but the figures for gross
rentals are more accurate :

Gross rental of agricultural land £4,203
Gross rental of osier beds . . . . . . £81 10s.
(A proportion of approximately 51½ to 1)

On neighbouring estates of 2,223 acres, 965 acres, and
3,234 acres, the acreage under willows is 6, 1, and 0, respectively.

In this district the quantity of willows grown is not
sufficient to supply all the rods needed by the local basket-
makers, who would prefer to cultivate their own material if
they could obtain land within easy reach of their workshops,
but who deplore the waste of time involved in going to and
from beds at a distance from the village.

Farndon, near Newark.

Agricultural land . . . . . . about 1,727
Osier beds . . . . . about   22 acres
(A proportion of 78½ to 1)
Average rateable value of agricultural land, 35s. per acre.
Average rateable value of osier beds, 47s. 6d. per acre.

Elston, near Newark.

Agricultural land . . . . . about 1,549 acres
Osier beds . . . . . about   31 acres
(A proportion of 50 to 1)
Gross rental of agricultural land . . . £1,619 15s. 3d.
Gross rental of osier beds . . . . £54 0s. 0d.
(A proportion of approximately 30 to 1)

East Stoke, near Newark

Agricultural land . . . . . about 1,550 acres
Osier beds . . . . . about   16 acres
(A proportion of approximately 97 to 1)
Gross rental of agricultural land . . . £1,634 0s. 0d.
Gross rental of osier beds . . . . £41 10s. 0d.
(A proportion of nearly 39½ to 1)

The basket-making firms in the Trent Valley district are of all sizes, comprising from three hundred workers to a single one.[1] There are large firms in the towns of Nottingham, Derby, Newark, and Leicester, and in the village of Thurmaston, near the last town, and smaller ones in Loughborough and the villages of Castle Donington (where there are as many as seven makers), Sutton-on-Trent, East Leake, Sutton (near East Retford), and Spondon (near Derby). A large firm in Grantham and a smaller one in Bourne (Lincs.), although beyond the Trent Valley district, really belong to this group.

The chief output of this district is cane and wicker furniture, both of the best quality and also of a cheaper type ; large numbers of shopping and other light fancy baskets in flat skein work are also made, and other products include large baskets for General Post Office contracts and fish baskets for Grimsby. The making of wicker furniture and fancy baskets is most directly dependant upon the locally grown material, great quantities of the finest rods, stained by the ' buffing ' process to the tan colour generally preferred for this work, being used. The development of the skilled craftsmanship necessary for this kind of basketry, and the large scale organization of the firms in this district, has led to the introduction of the cane furniture-making, for which the same high level of skill and the same large organization for wholesale selling is required.

The Mawdesley district, in Lancashire, somewhat resembles that of the Trent valley in the high level of osier cultivation. Two growers have plots of a hundred and fifty acres each, and a third has fifty acres. Although the acreage under willows is large, the district in which they occur is a small one, with a radius of not more than ten miles around the village of Mawdesley, near Ormskirk. The soil is particularly adapted for one variety, ' Dicky Meadowes ', which is difficult to grow elsewhere. The opinion of one expert, who has grown willows here all through his life, and whose father did the same, is that there is no peculiar excellence in the soil, or, indeed, any native superiority in the place which cannot be matched in many other places in England.

---

[1] Firms in large industrial towns, such as Nottingham and Derby, would not ordinarily be included amongst rural industries, but in this case they are so intimately connected with the osier cultivation of the district that they cannot be ignored. Basket-making firms in other large towns, which have no particular connexion with local rural conditions, have not been included in the survey.

The distinguishing characteristic of Mawdesley is that willow growing here is already a traditional occupation, and from childhood each man assimilates the requisite knowledge. This is particularly important for the cultivation of ' Dicks ', which are very slow starters. The nature of the basket-making industry here is directly determined by the variety of osiers grown ; shopping baskets and other light baskets, for which the ' Dicks ' are particularly suitable, are almost the only kinds made.

The osier-growing district next in importance to these two is in Somerset, where withies (as they are generally called here) are grown on the flats of Sedgemoor and in the adjoining river meadows along the banks of the Parrett, between Martock and Bridgwater. The whole of Sedgemoor —which was a swamp until it was reclaimed by a great drainage scheme—is peaty, and on the north side there are mosses where peat cutting is the main industry. A network of straight dykes, or ' rhines ', conducts the water to the Parrett, and attention has to be paid to these to keep them clear of weeds. Official estimates give the area under withies in Somerset as two thousand acres. The basketry industry here takes the form of wicker furniture work ; it is carried on in and around Bridgwater—where about two hundred men and a hundred and fifty women are employed— and at North Petherton. The Somerset osiers are inferior to those grown in the Trent valley, and the basket work is of a correspondingly lower grade.

These three districts, together with the Thames valley,[1] are famous as centres of osier-growing and basket-making. In other parts of England willows are grown in comparatively small quantities to meet the local basket-makers' demand for material. In these cases the growers seldom give to their crops the careful and intensive cultivation common in the more important districts already described, aiming only at supplying a sufficient quantity of useable material at low cost for local use.

In the Fen Country of the East Midlands (including the Isle of Ely and other parts of Cambridgeshire and Hunts.), there was an important industry for the making of baskets used for packing the fruit and vegetables so extensively grown here. Only a small proportion of the baskets so used are now made locally, the industry having greatly decreased in recent years. Baskets for the harvesting of the potato and carrot crops are still supplied chiefly by local makers.

[1] Dealt with in *Rural Industries around Oxford*—K. S. Woods.

Although the baskets used for the marketing of fruit and vegetables are the property of the salesmen, and most of the crops of this district are destined for the markets of London or of the northern industrial towns, in cases where English baskets are used it has proved most convenient to have them made in the vicinity of the orchards. Thus it happens that in the Fen District numbers of basket-makers are found in the villages round which the cultivation of fruit, potatoes, or carrots, or market-gardening is carried on. Cottenham, Ely, Somersham, Earith, Chatteris, and St. Neot's are centres of the basket-making industry, which also exists to a smaller extent in Soham, Haddenham, Histon, Buckden, and March. Several of these firms are on a fairly large scale, but there are, in addition, a number of scattered makers who are also fruit growers, or agents, often small-holders, or with basket-making carried on as a supplementary industry. One large firm of fruit growers and preserve manufacturers cultivates a few acres of osiers on the 'washes', or borders of the river, in Burnt Fen and Sedge Fen, the main consideration in this case being the suitability of the land for the crop; two or three men are employed to make fruit sieves for use in the firm's orchards. Osiers are grown to a fairly large extent throughout the district. Cambridgeshire, including the Isle of Ely, was estimated in 1918 to have one hundred and fifty acres, and there are about seventy or eighty acres more under cultivation in Huntingdonshire, and perhaps a further fifty acres running wild. One Ely grower has a plot of fifty-five acres, and a large proportion of the crop from this bed was formerly used by a big basket-making firm whose workshops, now closed, stand by the river, opposite to the bed. Another grower, at St. Ives, has a forty acre holt, but the rest of the acreage in the district is in small plots along the valleys of the Nene, the Ouse and its tributaries, the Cam, and the Ivel. In the Soke of Peterborough there are forty acres, all the property of one grower, whose chief output in baskets, however, consists of work for General Post Office contracts, and not of fruit or potato baskets.

The market-gardening industry of Bedfordshire has determined the situation of basket-making firms in Leighton Buzzard, Biggleswade, and Bedford, of which those in the two former towns have their own willow holts, although the total acreage of osiers in this country is under fifty acres.

In Gloucestershire, Worcestershire, and the south of Warwickshire, there are many basket-makers whose *raison d'être* is the existence of orchards and market-gardens in the locality. In this district the produce is chiefly sold in the neighbouring markets of Gloucester, Cheltenham, Evesham, and Worcester, or in Birmingham. The exact location of the basket industries within this district is sometimes dependant on the supply of osiers, as at Apperley, Westbury-on-Severn, Maisemore, and Quedgeley, all on the banks of the Severn, where there are beds of from five to fifty acres in extent. In some cases the basket-maker has settled near the orchards, as in the Pershore and Evesham districts ; three basket-makers in the latter town own osier beds in the neighbourhood. Other makers find it more convenient to have their workshops in the town where the markets for the fruit and garden produce are held, as at Stratford-on-Avon and Gloucester. There has recently been a great decrease in the basket-making industry in this, as in other fruit-growing districts, and the firms, when visited in 1922 and 1923, were working on a small scale. In addition to the osier-beds near the basket workshops, there is one at Ripple, on the Severn, of sixteen acres, and others in the Golden Valley, and near Cirencester and Chipping Sodbury. Most of them are owned by basket-makers. A Gloucester maker claimed that he had a hundred acres, scattered all over the country, but this seemed to mean merely that he buys the crops off that number of acres from several small growers, and perhaps gives them a little advice as to the varieties to be planted. This arrangement seems to be a common one in Gloucestershire. In Worcestershire there are only from fifty to sixty acres under osiers throughout the county. In South Warwickshire, between Warwick, Stratford, and Alcester, the area under willows was computed in 1918 to be seventy-one acres, but of this, twenty-seven acres were derelict even then, and the position in 1923, when the district was surveyed, was still worse.

In South Cornwall the basket industry is definitely related to the market-gardening carried on in the locality, and is concentrated within a small area. There are a few acres grown near Penzance, and some neglected beds to the west of the town. There are about twenty workshops in the towns and a few villages, with a total of not more than forty men engaged in the industry. The specialities of the district are broccoli crates and potato baskets. The osiers grown in this county, called locally ' English old oak ', with sarcastic reference to their strong, harsh nature, are only suited to the roughest work. Both in Dorset and in

Cornwall a few willows are also grown by fishermen, on clay patches on the tops of the cliffs, the rods being used for making crab and lobster pots.

In the fruit-growing districts of Kent there used to be many makers of bushel sieves and other baskets used for packing fruit, but foreign competition has been even more severely felt here than in the west of England, probably owing to the fact that immense numbers of Dutch baskets are shipped direct to the port of London and are particularly accessible to the Covent Garden Market salesmen, who buy most of the produce of the Kentish orchards. Fruit sieves are still made in Sandwich and Swanley, and were also produced until recently in Maidstone.

There are small groups of basket-makers, whose situation is determined by the existence of local fruit-growing and market-gardening industries, in the Lea valley, and in the Thames valley around Staines and Feltham. A few osiers are grown in the Lea valley. Several firms in Watford, Berkhamsted, and elsewhere, make special baskets for the water-cress growers who supply the London market.

In districts other than those already mentioned basket-making is carried on by numerous small firms, generally situated in the villages or market towns, often consisting of only one or two workers, who are not such specialists as those who make the Trent valley osiers into furniture or shopping baskets, or the makers of fruit pots or sieves. They are to be found in the greatest numbers in Yorkshire, Lincolnshire, and East Anglia, and more sparsely in other counties. In the East and West Ridings of Yorkshire there are about twenty makers, chiefly concentrated in the Plain of York, Selby being the centre both of the potato-growing area and of the basket industry, which is here connected with it, although the makers also do all kinds of other general work. According to official estimates, there were three hundred acres of willows grown in the East and West Ridings of Yorkshire in 1918, nearly all in this particular district, but in 1922 there did not seem to be more than one hundred acres under cultivation. There are several small garths (as the willow beds are called here), of from three to ten acres around Selby, the willows being grown both for the use of the basket-makers who own them and for sale to others ; at Aberford there are twelve acres, in small strips by a stream, and at Tadcaster some big garths. In the North Riding there are makers at Darlington and Yarm, Whitby and Malton, and willow garths at Darlington

and Malton. There are also one or two others in the market
towns of the East and West Ridings, beyond the Selby
district, and in Hull. At Burton-in-Lonsdale, on the
Lancashire border, a few osiers are grown to make wicker
covers for the large jars produced by a local pottery.

In the Lindsey and Kesteven divisions of Lincolnshire
there are about a dozen makers in the market towns, supplying chiefly the needs of local farmers, whilst the port of
Grimsby provides occupation for several makers of fish and
coal baskets. There are a number of small garths in the
county, all owned by basket-makers, one of whom has
twelve acres in Bassingham Fen, and sells green rods to
Nottinghamshire. The large garths near Grantham have
already been mentioned in connexion with the Trent Valley
district.

In Norfolk there are about thirty makers who, except for
those situated in Yarmouth, Lowestoft, King's Lynn, and
Norwich, are to be found in the smaller towns and even in
the remotest villages. Probably the number of baskets
made in this county is no greater than the total output of
Lincolnshire or Yorkshire, the carrying on of basket-making
as a part-time industry by thatchers, smallholders, and
others, being a feature of the district. Another local characteristic is that few of the makers grow their own rods,
although there are about fifty acres of cultivated osiers in
the county, planted by farmers, who sell the crops to the
basket-makers. There is also an indefinite area, estimated
as ten times the area of the cultivated beds, planted with
willows for the purpose of providing cover for game. These
rods also are used to some extent by local basket-makers.
The Norfolk rods are of poor quality, owing to the fact that
they are not cultivated either by expert willow growers or
by the basket-makers themselves, and the local basket-work
is correspondingly rough.

There are about half a dozen makers in Suffolk, and there
are osier-beds, estimated at one hundred acres in extent,
near Stowmarket, with another hundred acres scattered
about the county. In Essex there are about the same
number of basket-makers, most of them in the large towns,
but there are only three or four plots of basket willows.
Timber willows for cricket bats are grown extensively in
this county.

Special local demands, other than the ordinary ones of
farmers for feeding skeps, scuttles, &c., of tradesmen for
delivery baskets, and of private people for shopping baskets,

are those provided by factories. In the industrial towns of
the West Riding of Yorkshire there are many makers of the
big, heavy skeps used in the textile mills, and several basket-
makers in Northamptonshire do a considerable amount of
work for the boot factories, as well as for farmers and other
customers. None of these workers use locally grown willows.
A firm near Bakewell makes big cane baskets for the hosiery
factories of Derby and Belper. Cane, of course, is an
imported material.

Of the counties not yet mentioned, Northumberland,
Westmorland, Cumberland, Cheshire, Shropshire, and
Staffordshire have only one or two basket-makers each,
in the rural districts. In Durham, which is almost entirely
industrialized, not a single maker was found in the small
rural area which remains, owing to the fact that the farming
carried on there is not of the type which makes much use
of baskets. The existence of each of the small single industries found in Northumberland and Westmorland seemed
due rather more to the fact that the man was an osier-grower
on a small scale, and made baskets to use up his rods, than
to any great local demand for his wares. In fact, the former
maker, at Berwick, seems almost to be a Trent valley man
gone astray, for he is an artist in osier-growing, and makes
baskets as a penance. In Cumberland, the only willows
grown are in a few uncultivated beds beside a railway line.
The rods from one or two beds along the Cheshire rivers are
used locally in their brown (unpeeled) state for rough work,
rods for finer work being easily obtained from Birmingham
or Liverpool merchants.

In the south-western counties, where there is more arable
farming, basket-making is more flourishing, and several
makers are found in market centres and in Plymouth, Exeter,
and Bristol. In Dorset, Wilts., and Hants there are a few
old osier-beds, on swampy ground by rivers, the rods being
used only for ' brown ' work by local makers.

In Surrey and Sussex there are a number of makers in the
towns. Few osiers are grown in these counties. The fathers
of present day basket-makers at Rye, Hastings, and East-
bourne spoke of having used locally grown rods, but the sons
now buy their material from Somerset. There are osier-beds
near Lewes and Guildford, and a few osiers are grown on
Battle sewage farm. Another sewage farm on which osiers
have been planted is that at Billing, in Northamptonshire,
in which county there are less than twenty acres altogether.
In other counties, in addition to the beds which have been

mentioned, there are a number of acres planted with willows
rather as a means of utilizing waste wet patches of ground
for purposes of cover, than as a serious attempt to produce
rods suitable for basketry.

In the market-gardening and fruit-growing areas there are,
in addition to the firms which specialize in baskets for use
in this connexion, a certain number of makers in the towns
who only do the ordinary general work.   There are also to
be found in some rural areas a few firms who manufacture
some particular kind of basket for the wholesale market, such
as a firm in the Barnstaple district which makes shopping
and other light baskets for the Domestic Bazaar Company,
and one in a village of Cambridgeshire which employs several
girls on bicycle baskets.

II. *The Organization of the Osier-growing and Basket-making Industries.*

The osier-growing and basket-making industries are, as
might be expected from their close relationship, often carried
on side by side, by the same firms or individuals, who make
up in their own workshops a part or all of the osiers grown
in their holts.   This is the system generally in force in the
Trent Valley district.   There are also a certain number of
firms and individual workers who are only osier-growers or
only basket-makers, but these are for the most part of less
importance in the industry.   From the point of view of
organization, those carrying on the two industries may be
divided into six classes, as follows :

1. Those (large firms for the most part) for whom the
cultivation of osiers is of primary importance, basket-making
being a subsidiary industry, although often carried out on
an extensive scale.   As a rule these growers also sell a considerable quantity of rods.   This class includes most of the
Trent Valley firms.

2. Large growers, who are not basket-makers, but who
supply the wholesale market with rods.   These are to be
found chiefly in Somerset.

3. Those who are primarily basket-makers and who cultivate osiers merely for the sake of providing themselves with
material.   This class includes the majority of the rural basket-
makers.

4. Growers who supply only a local market.   This is a very
large class, comprising men who grow small plots of osiers
and sell the crops to local makers.

5. Basket-makers, on a small scale for the most part, who grow no osiers themselves, but who buy rods or standing crops from local growers or who depend on dealers for their supply. Many basket-makers obtain their material by all these methods.

6. Firms or individuals, other than osier-growers, who carry on basket-making in conjunction with some other industry or trade.

Class 1. In the Trent Valley most of the willow-growers own basketry workshops, and although basket-making has grown up here as a subsidiary industry, it is, nevertheless, highly organized and carried out on a large scale, and the work done is of the finest quality. Many of the workshops are in the large towns, and from twenty to one hundred workers, and in one or two cases up to three hundred, are employed in each. There are sometimes as many as fourteen men employed even by a village firm. The organization of the larger firms is of the factory type, each worker being a specialist in some one branch of the craft.

In connexion with some of the Trent Valley firms there is a system of family or home work, unusual in the basket-making industry. In the village of Castle Donington a number of small growers have found it convenient to work exclusively on contracts for large Nottingham firms, their work being of a type more easily disposed of through whole-sale dealers. The industry has been carried on in the same way by these families for generations. Around Grantham there are about thirty home workers employed on contracts for a firm in that town. They formerly made potato baskets, but the increased imports of Belgian baskets have rendered this form of production unprofitable, and they have been put on to other work, such as the making of dog baskets. These are not growers, as are the Castle Donington workers, their position corresponding rather to that of the ordinary factory outworker.

A feature of the Trent Valley firms is the number of osier-beds of very large size owned by them, although there are also many small growers. The sizes of the beds range from half an acre up to a hundred acres. Many of the firms comprise all branches of both industries, from the cultivation of osiers and the preparation of the rods by peeling and buffing, to the making of baskets and wholesale dealing both in rods and in basketry work. Only a small proportion of the Trent Valley rods are used locally, this district being the source from which basket-makers all over England, particularly the town workers, obtain rods of fine quality.

The small district around Mawdesley (Lancs.) somewhat resembles the Trent Valley area in its organization. Two growers here own beds of one hundred and fifty acres each, and each employs about thirty basket-makers. Although Mawdesley is of considerable importance by reason of the high standard of osier cultivation here, it does not supply such a large general market as does the Trent Valley, because the Mawdesley growers specialize in one particular variety of osier, 'Dicky Meadowes', which is suitable only for certain kinds of work. For particularly fine work, however, these rods are ordered from all parts of England.

Beyond the Trent Valley and Mawdesley districts this type of osier-grower for the wholesale market, who also owns basketry workshops, is hardly to be found. In Somerset the two industries are carried on separately in most cases, although there are also combined firms, notably one which owns a wicker-furniture factory in Bridgwater, employing seventy journeymen, and osier-beds and storehouses in Gloucestershire and Worcestershire. During the war, when the rush plait used for decoration in wicker-furniture work could no longer be obtained from Belgium, the firm rented cutting rights for rushes in the river Avon and had the rush plait made up for them. This firm, like those of the Trent Valley, comprises in itself the complete machinery for all branches of the industry, from the cultivation of the raw material to the sale of the finished product.

In other districts the cultivation of osiers is usually only incidental to basket-making.

Class 2. Growers for the wholesale market who are not also basket-makers are to be found chiefly in Somerset, and this county has its own characteristic type of organization in the osier-growing industry. Many of the growers on Sedgemoor, who supply rods to the Bridgwater wicker-furniture makers as well as to a wider market, own large beds, and it is a local custom to let out small plots cheaply to men who will cultivate them well, under the condition that the owner shall have the option of buying the rods at the current market price. These small cultivators are, for the most part, the settlers who have built themselves cottages on the 'droves'—the raised tracks running along the dykes of Sedgemoor. Many of them also work at busy seasons on the beds of the bigger growers. The women take their share of work and interest in the industry, 'stripping' (peeling) the rods in their homes during the winter. Some of the men also make baskets as a spare-time industry. The system seems to work well, giving the men a proprietary interest in the beds, with the result that they work hard ; the moral and intellectual standard of the people, who are said to have been rough and illiterate some thirty years ago, has improved with the development of the industry.

Class 3. The third class—of those who are primarily basket-makers, cultivating osiers for their own use—comprises a great number of rural basket-makers, both those who do general work and those who make fruit pots and sieves. In the West Country and in the East Midlands quite 50 per cent. of the basket-makers have their own osier-beds.

The firms, which are to be found in country towns and villages in nearly every county, making shopping baskets and baskets for agricultural use, almost entirely for local sale, are small ; sometimes three men, or fewer, are employed, more often a father and son, or two or three brothers, work together. One rural firm in South Cornwall employs as many as ten men, but this is unusual. There are many single-handed rural basket-makers, and others employ a man only occasionally in a busy season.

The usual size of the holt cultivated by the village or country town basket-maker is from two to six acres, and this provides him with nearly all that he needs ; sometimes it is as large as from ten to fifteen acres, and in this case he probably sells some surplus rods. The firm near Peterborough, which makes baskets for the General Post Office, and which owns a forty-acre holt, may perhaps be considered as belonging to this class, since they grow rods mainly for their own use, although in other respects they are of a different type.

The firms making fruit pots and sieves are usually larger than those doing general agricultural work. Since these baskets for fruit are always needed in considerable quantities, the making of them cannot be undertaken by the single-handed village basket-maker. Some of the fruit pot and sieve firms employ fifty men or more (although since the war the numbers have been greatly reduced), and there are smaller firms, comprising only about half a dozen journeymen. It is usually the latter firms which own osier holts and cultivate rods for their own use.

The usual system amongst the small rural basket-makers is for work in the holts to be alternated with basket-making in the workshop, according to the season. This system is also carried out in some cases by the larger firms who make fruit and market-garden baskets. The orders for these baskets come in with the new year in a good trade season, or not until just before the summer in a bad one. As a rule the baskets are only made to order, as it is too risky to make for stock. Thus, when orders are scarce, the men can work on the beds during the winter and, in any case, unless they are busy making potato baskets, they will not have much to do in the workshop after August, and are sure to be free again to begin cutting in November. The greatest difficulty is to get the beds weeded in the spring, when the men will be busy on the fruit pots. The planning of the work depends, of course, on the kinds of baskets made ; if a man is occupied in making potato baskets and feeding-skeps, he may not have time to give to osier cutting in the late autumn and winter, and in this case he may employ a cutter. The system perhaps leads to a somewhat erratic cultivation of the beds, which may be neglected at an important season, but, since the rods are to be used by the grower himself, and the quality of his work depends upon them, he will care for them as well as he is able. The standard of cultivation of the beds belonging to basket-makers was noticeable in several districts as considerably above that of the holts belonging to farmers, who grow willows in order to use up waste patches of land, and who, although they rely upon selling the crops to local basket-makers, give the rods very little care. Many rural basket-makers, however, use the rods grown on their own holts only for the rougher work, such as agricultural baskets, whilst for any finer work which they may do, such as baskets for shopping and for household purposes, they buy bundles of white and buff rods, usually from Somerset. A maker of wicker furniture was met with who only cut the growths of two years, known as ' sticks ' and used as the framework of chairs, from his own holt, buying all the other material which he needed.

Class 4. The fourth class, that of growers who supply only a local market, is of little importance, since they usually cultivate their holts with very indifferent care and can hardly be considered seriously as growers. As a rule they do not like to undertake the troublesome business of cutting and preparing the rods, but sell them as a standing crop to the basket-maker. This method saves the grower from the trouble of sorting the rods, storing them and dealing with a number of buyers, but any grower who takes a real interest in his osier holt would be reluctant to adopt this method, because the buyer may employ an indifferent cutter who, by careless or inexpert work, may damage the heads.

The buyer also usually dislikes this method of obtaining
raw material. As a rule it is only the small-scale country
worker, who does none of the finer work for which special
varieties of rods are essential, and who has family labour
available for peeling and sorting, who finds it more economical to buy the standing crop of a local grower.

It is not surprising that this method of obtaining raw
material is commonest in the areas where the standard of
osier-growing is low and where the basket work is chiefly
of the roughest kind. In Gloucestershire and East Anglia
the system of buying a standing crop seems to be the general
rule. Basket-makers in these districts say that it is almost
impossible to rent or buy suitable land on which to grow
their own crops. There is a general complaint that the
farmers and landowners, who are the growers here, know
little about the varieties of osiers and the cultivation needed,
and are not very willing to take advice. They are apt to
account for the poor quality of the rods produced by a vague
generalization as to the unsuitability of the local soil and
climate for osier-growing. Others, who have probably never
seen a well-kept osier-bed, will maintain that osiers need no
cultivation. In Gloucestershire, one basket-maker, who
obtains his material from a neighbouring estate, stated that
he is often consulted as to varieties to be planted and
methods of cultivation, and occasionally he sends some of
his own men to work in the beds.

In Warwickshire, in 1923, many basket-makers who in
normal times would have bought rods from Somerset, were
trying to economize by buying standing crops from local
beds which had been seriously neglected during the war.
This plan involved less expenditure, and there were so few
orders for baskets that the men could give their time to the
cutting and peeling of the rods. The material, however,
was poor, and only fit for rough work. The high cost of
labour had caused the owners to neglect the beds to such
an extent that in 1923, when the price of rods had fallen
and was still falling, it would not have paid them to clean
the beds, cut and prepare the rods, and sell them by the
bundle, as they would have done in normal times. They
were therefore glad to dispose of the standing crops at a low
price.

There are a few exceptional cases of growers for a local
market whose holts are well cultivated. At Ely there is
a fifty-five acre holt, of which nearly all the produce was
formerly utilized in the big basketry workshops of the

opposite side of the river. In 1922, when this district was surveyed, the holt was still clean and well cared for, although the workshops were shut. In this case the rods would be good enough for sale in the wholesale market, and in any case a grower on such a large scale must always have sold a certain amount of material in this way, although the holt was originally planted in order to supply the Ely workshops, where fruit sieves were made. In Cambridgeshire, a small-holder was heard of who devoted the whole of his holding to osier cultivation, and was said to find a good market amongst local basket-makers.

Class 5. The fifth class (of basket-makers who do not themselves grow any osiers), includes the rural workers who buy from the growers in class 4 (see above), the ' garret men ' in country towns, and many urban firms which do not come within the scope of this survey. The wicker-furniture factories of Somerset, however, should be mentioned, as they are closely connected with the osier-growing industry of Sedgemoor, whence they obtain their supplies of material. These firms are concentrated in and around Bridgwater ; one, which also owns osier beds, has already been mentioned in class 1 ; two others in 1921 each employed fifty workers. There is a smaller firm in a Cambridgeshire village which employs several girls to make bicycle baskets for the whole-sale trade, but it is unusual to find a basket industry of this type in a village. Since rods only of one particular quality are needed, and those rather fine, such a firm finds it more convenient to buy rods already prepared than to cultivate their own holt.

The ' garret men ' are single-handed workers in the towns, who have not the advantage enjoyed by the majority of the village makers of being able to cultivate their own osier-beds, or at least to obtain their material cheaply by buying a crop from a local grower.

Class 6. The sixth class, comprising firms and individuals who carry on basketry in conjunction with some other industry, is a miscellaneous one. Basket-making on a large or small scale is often carried on by shops which sell fancy goods, toys, furniture, or mats and rugs. They may employ one or two men to make baskets for sale in the shop and to do repairing work, or baskets may be made in considerable quantities for the wholesale trade. Similarly, a basket-maker in a market town often keeps a small shop, mainly for the sale of his own goods, in which he stocks a few other articles, sometimes including imported baskets of the lighter varieties, or rope and twine. Basket-making and rope-making carried on in conjunction were met with in two or three instances. Basketry is also carried on by certain dealers in or manufacturers of tools and materials for basketry and other handicraft work.

Some firms employ a few men to make baskets for a special purpose of their own, such as the covering with wicker work of large spirit and pickle jars, for which a basket-maker may be employed at a pottery. Some produce salesmen in Gloucestershire and Warwickshire have sieves, pots, and other baskets for fruit and market-garden produce made on their premises, although this practice is becoming less usual as the imported pots and sieves tend to oust the home-made kind. One salesman was met with who found it profitable to employ men to make certain baskets of unusual shapes and sizes, such as butter baskets and fell crates, which cannot be bought in large quantities from importers. In 1923 this salesman found that he did not need sufficient of these to keep the two men busy all the year round, so they filled up their time by making pots, which, however, cost the salesman more than the Dutch ones which he buys in great quantities. In the Fen Country there are a number of salesmen or agents who cultivate small osier holts and employ a few men making sieves and other baskets for fruit.

There are many rural basket-makers working single-handed who also carry on some other industry. Fishermen on the south coast make their own lobster and crab pots. Smallholders, especially in Norfolk and the Fen Country, find basket-making a convenient industry for the slack winter months. On the Norfolk Broads, where reeds grow plentifully and reed thatch is much in use, many thatchers carry on basket-making as an alternative industry for wet weather, when thatching cannot be done.

An organization of basket-makers has been in existence since very early times, the Basket-makers' Company being one of the oldest of the Craft Guilds. The modern organi-zation is the Employers' Federation of Cane and Willow Workers' Associations of Great Britain and Ireland, of which the affiliated associations are those of London, Lanca-shire and Cheshire, Yorkshire, the Midland Counties, and the West of England and South Wales. These associations include many of the osier-growers, who have no separate organization. Matters which affect the basket-making in-dustry are usually of equal importance to the willow-growers,

and difficult questions with regard to either trade usually
arise in connexion with the basket industry, which is more
complicated in its commercial aspect than the other. The
Cane and Willow Workers' Association, where it operates,
fixes the selling prices of rods as well as the piece rates for
basket-making.

The men are organized in the British Amalgamated Union
of Basket-makers. Organization has advanced rapidly in
recent years, but there are many difficulties to be faced in
these industries, and the rural workers still remain almost
unorganized. Owing to the simple nature of the industry,
the fact that the plant and tools needed are comparatively
inexpensive, and that a business can be started with a small
supply of material, it is easy for journeymen to become
masters, and so the latter are largely recruited from a poorly
educated class, amongst whom organization is difficult.
A large number of rural basket-makers are neither employers
nor employees, but men working by themselves.

In South Cornwall there is a local branch of the Basket-
makers' Union and also an independent Masters' Association.
Twenty-one out of the twenty-six journeymen in Penzance
belong to the former ; the remaining members include one
boy and the sons or brothers of the master makers. The
weakness of the organization in the West of England is
notable ; some of the Gloucestershire journeymen belong to
a branch of the union of which the secretary is as far distant
as Derby. The rates paid for this district are generally
below those fixed for the Midland Counties. The industry
in the Trent Valley district is probably the best organized
in England. The East Midlands seem to be almost totally
lacking in any organization, and the same is true of the
rural makers of Lincolnshire, East Anglia, and the south-
eastern counties, and of the more scattered rural makers in
the other counties.

Organization of the trade, in addition to regulating the
rates of pay, standard of work, and terms of apprenticeship,
might help to bring the small isolated makers into touch
with a wider market. A village basket-maker is chiefly con-
versant with the locally used varieties of baskets, but if
there is a slackening of the demand for these he does not
know how to find a fresh outlet for his goods nor what
kinds may command a sale in another market. It is often
the case that one of these small rural makers is, with difficulty, earning the scantiest livelihood by making baskets
for local farmers, whilst another, within a few miles of him,

has quite a profitable industry for the supply of some special demand, and one which is capable of extension.

III. *The Marketing of Rods and the Supply of Material to Basket-makers.*

Many basket-makers who cultivate their own holts also need to obtain rods from other sources. A country basket-maker whose business is on a small scale and who does none of the finer work for which special varieties are essential, may find it more economical to buy the crop of a local grower, re-selling to other makers any surplus material that is unsuited to his use, than to buy bundles of rods from a dealer. Particularly when the holt is near the workshop, when the basket-maker or one of his employees is competent to undertake the cutting of the crop, and where family labour is available for peeling and there is room for storage, does this method of obtaining material find favour. In other cases, however, it is disliked by the basket-maker, and may only be adopted for the sake of economy when ready money is short.

Basket-makers who produce a great variety of work for the individual demands of private customers, particularly the town makers, find it more economical and less trouble-some to buy rods from the dealers, who can supply white or buff rods of the different kinds needed for different work, properly sorted and made up into bundles.

In the more important osier-growing districts, such as the Trent Valley, Sedgemoor, and Mawdesley, the local makers use a large quantity of the rods grown in the neighbourhood, although the supply, in these cases, far exceeds the local demand, so there are many other buyers. These districts are the main sources of supply to basket-makers throughout the country. The Trent Valley rods, of better quality and more expensive than other English varieties, are little used by rural makers, being more suitable for the finer work done by town firms for the wholesale market, but some country makers, who also do a little of the lighter work, buy Notting-hamshire rods in small quantities for this purpose. The Somerset osiers are particularly suitable for the rural basket-maker, being cheaper than Nottinghamshire rods, and although not of such fine quality, good enough for all but the finest work. Many country basket-makers who can obtain uncultivated rods from local estates use these for the rough brown work, and buy from Somerset such peeled and buffed rods as they may need. There is an interchange of material between Somerset and some other districts, Worcestershire growers, for example, sending rods to Somerset and buying others there.

In other districts than these three main ones, rods are grown almost exclusively for local use, although a few cases were heard of in which growers produced a sufficient quantity to supply a market beyond their own immediate locality. A large grower in Huntingdonshire and another in Bedfordshire peel and buff their best rods for the wholesale market, selling the others for local use in their brown state.

In Gloucestershire, the East Midlands, and Lincolnshire a considerable proportion of the rods used are grown by the basket-makers themselves or bought by them from local growers. In Warwickshire few of the basket-makers have willow holts of their own, but they buy a good deal of their material from neighbouring growers. The basket-makers of Cornwall, Dorset, Wiltshire, Hampshire, the Isle of Wight, and Worcestershire, obtain their rods chiefly from Somerset and Berkshire ; Gloucestershire makers use Somerset rods for their finer work, and Somerset also supplies most of the material used in the rural districts in East Anglia and the south-eastern counties. For rough agricultural baskets, some Norfolk makers buy rods from the Fen Country.

Foreign rods do not seem to be used very largely by rural basket-makers, although large quantities of them are imported. Many makers describe them as ' poor stuff ', and undoubtedly some of the imported material is decidedly inferior to the English varieties. The Dutch are reputed to grow rods of good quality, but seem to keep the best for home use. Some excellent material comes from France, but this is of the kind used by makers of fancy baskets. Belgian rods are sometimes preferred to English, rather because they are better sorted than on account of any superiority of quality.

A few cases of the export of Somerset rods to other countries were heard of, but they were probably casual shipments to meet abnormal conditions. Immediately after the war an American firm, which had formerly bought from France or Belgium, did a certain amount of trade with this district, and withies were also sent to Canada to relatives of the growers at home. Before the war a small quantity of rods was sent to Germany, but this trade seems unlikely to revive.

In some cases there seems to be an unfortunate lack of co-operation between basket-makers and willow-growers. In

Yorkshire, in 1922, several makers complained of the difficulty of obtaining rods, speaking even of a shortage, whilst
growers in the same district had difficulty in disposing of
their crops.   Makers complain that the growers do not
sufficiently study the needs of the users of the rods.   The
smaller growers often describe their crops vaguely as ' all
kinds mixed ', and obviously take little trouble to select
the best varieties and to keep them separate.   They also
fail to sort the rods in such a way that a bundle shall contain
those of one size and one variety only.   These criticisms
apply chiefly to the farmers and others who grow willows
as a side-line, and to the districts in which willow-growing
is not carried on very extensively.   In Yorkshire one or
two growers and basket-makers had developed a profitable
business as middlemen, buying crops of willows, sorting and
preparing them, and re-selling.   The holts from which they
bought their material and the customers to whom they sold
it were all situated within quite a small area, and the fact
that there was an opening for such middlemen seems to
indicate a failure on the part of the growers and users of
rods to co-operate, at a time when both classes were suffering from slackness of trade and cut prices, and therefore could
ill afford to share their profits with a third person.

Complaints about the sorting and packing of rods are also
made with regard to the Somerset withies, but in this case
they apply chiefly to the green or brown (unpeeled) rods.
Somerset osiers are measured by bolts, not by weight, and
the bolts vary in size.   The green rods (those just cut) are
tied in ' half-bundles '.   When the rods have been sorted
and cleared of weeds before being bundled, the half-bundle
measures 2 ft. 6 in. in girth, at 4 in. from the butt ends.
Two half-bundles, when peeled, make one bundle or bolt of
white rods, this bolt measuring 3 ft. 1 in.   Formerly, the
standard measurement of the bolt was 3 ft. 2 in.   About
two hundred of these bolts now go to a ton.   If the green
rods are tied up unsorted and mixed with weeds, the half
bundle measures 3 ft. 3 in., and about three of these half
bundles go to one bolt of peeled rods.   The ratio of peeled
to unpeeled rods is variable, depending upon the thickness
of the bark and the size of the rod.   There is more wastage
of peel on smaller rods.   Such variations in the size of the
bundles are naturally inconvenient to those who buy green
rods and, together with the Somerset growers' carelessness
in the matter of sorting, help to render the Somerset rods
unpopular in the Trent Valley, where the growers have a high

reputation for selling bundles containing the standard
quantity and of even quality. It is said that one bundle
of Somerset green withies may contain 15 per cent. less
material than another of nominally the same size, and a
basket-maker stated that the number of usable rods in two
bundles which he bought at the same time and for the same
price was 620 and 440 respectively—an even greater variation. Bolts in other parts of the country have varying
measurements, but as the rods are usually sold by weight,
this matters little. Ely bolts are 32 in. in girth, whilst
a neighbouring grower makes up bolts of 39½ in. In the
Trent Valley the bundles of green rods are called ' yards ',
measuring a yard in circumference.

Even the peeled rods are said to be badly sorted in
Somerset, so that buyers can never be certain of getting
exactly what they order, and may receive a certain amount
of material which is of no use for their particular work.
Again, when rods are sold by weight there is some uncertainty as to the amount of material which goes to make up
any given weight, this amount varying not only according
to the variety of rod, but also according to the growth of
the rods, their height and thickness, which differs according
to the season in which they are grown. The general opinion
in the industry, however, seems to be that it is more satisfactory to buy by weight, and that if only the rods are well
sorted, there can be little cause for complaint. It is in this
matter of sorting that the cheaper grades of English rods
are so inferior to foreign rods at the same price.

Amongst the osier-growers and basket-makers of the
Trent Valley district a system for the exchange of rods,
known locally as marketing, is in force. The grower with
a surplus seeks another man in the same predicament, and
if each finds that the other's surplus suits his requirements,
an exchange is effected. The value to be placed upon the
rods is said to be determined in these cases by offering them
to two or three different dealers and taking the average of
the prices offered. A system of this kind could only be
carried out in a district where the growers are known to one
another, and a spirit of confidence has been established in
an industry of fairly old standing.

Somerset also has its own characteristic system of marketing. Quantities of withies are auctioned annually here as
standing crops, and many of the cottagers buy small plats,
paying 10 per cent. deposit on purchase, the balance being
payable the following midsummer, when the rods have been

cut and sold. The auctioneer thus fulfills the function of
a bank by providing credit to the small men who could not
otherwise afford to buy a crop. Although the system is said
to be a costly one to these small buyers, it has given them
a certain independence. Many of the big Somerset growers
are also merchants, and sell their own crops and those of
other growers. Even before the war this had proved a
lucrative business, and during the war, when the prices of
rods rose rapidly, large profits are said to have been made.
The merchants often come in for a good deal of abuse from
the small growers, but there is no doubt that in this district
at least they have rendered a useful service to the industry
by bringing the growers into touch with wider markets and
thus increasing trade and raising the standard of cultivation.
They do not, like the Yorkshire middlemen, re-sell the rods
only in the same district. Not long ago the market for
Somerset osiers was almost entirely a local one, but now
a large number of basket-makers all over England, including
some in the Trent Valley district itself, depend mainly on
Somerset for their supplies.

The prices of rods rose during the war to an extent even
disproportionate to the increase in the cost of cultivation
and cutting. The prices continued to be high until 1920, in
which year the cost of some kinds of rods was five times the
pre-war price. In Nottinghamshire, rods which were sold
before the war for £4 a ton, fetched £20 a ton in 1920, and
the price of a kind sold for £40 a ton before the war was at
that time from £120 to £140. Another instance mentioned
was of brown rods which before the war cost from £2 to £5
a ton, and which were sold in 1919 for £14 a ton ; in exceptional cases £24 a ton had been asked for these rods. Dicky
Meadowes were sold green before the war for from £70 to
£80 a ton, and in 1920, at the annual auction at Mawdesley,
they fetched the same price. This kind of rod always fetches
a high price. The following list of prices actually paid at
different times for peeled Dicky Meadowes was given to
illustrate the rise from before the war to 1920 :

Pre-war .	. . . . .	28s. a cwt.
Jan. 1916	. . . .	48s. ,,
March 1917	. . . .	48s. ,,
May 1917	. . . .	52s. ,,
Sept. 1917	. . . .	65s. ,,
Feb. 1918	. . . .	90s. ,,
Jan. 1919	. . . .	190s. ,,
March 1920	. . . .	220s. ,,

In 1921 another buyer said that he had paid 250s. a cwt.

Prices paid for other kinds of white and buff rods in 1920 ranged from £70 to £130 a ton, according to quality, and from £112 to £120 a ton was said to be the usual price at this time for rods of average quality. A grower who sold his crop of green *Purpurea* for from £6 to £7 a ton before the war, sold it at £20 a ton in 1918, £50 a ton in 1919, and was asking £78 a ton in 1920. In Somerset it was said that whereas a hundred bundles of peeled rods were sold for £17 10s. before the war, similar rods fetched from 15s. to 20s. for *a single bundle* in 1920, and that brown rods, sold for 2s. a bundle before the war, were sold for from 9s. to 12s. a bundle in 1920.

A decline in these abnormal prices began after 1920, and during the next few years they fell constantly. Basket-makers, therefore, became reluctant to buy more than they required for their immediate use. One man was met with in 1923 who had bought a large quantity of buff rods some years before at the rate of 25s. a bundle. He expected to use them quickly on work which he was accustomed to do for wholesale orders but, with the general slump in trade, these orders soon dropped off, and for several years this man was only making baskets for local retail sale, for which buff rods were not often needed. Early in 1923 he still had on hand one bundle of the rods which he had bought at 25s., the price of which had by this time fallen again almost to the pre-war level of from 3s. to 4s. Another basket-maker who bought some white rods from Newark early in 1923 for £50 a ton, saw others of similar quality sold a few months later in a different place for £30 a ton. Occurrences of this sort naturally made basket-makers hesitate to buy more than the smallest possible quantity of rods at a time, and growers began to find difficulty in disposing of their crops before the prices fell. Small growers with little capital who failed to dispose of a crop early in the season would some-times, after the lapse of some months, sell their rods in a panic at a price far below the cost of production, being in need of ready money and alarmed at the prospect of a further reduction in prices when the new crops should come on the market.

Warwickshire growers, in 1922, said that they were selling in hundredweights where they usually sold in tons. The sudden drop in the prices of rods was hard on growers, as the cost of growing and preparing the rods fell more slowly. One Yorkshire grower declared in 1922 that the cost of preparing his crop for market that year was only 10s. a ton

less than in the previous year, 1*d.* a bundle off the wages
paid for peeling being the only reduction, whereas the selling
price was £21 a ton less.   Figures given in other districts
bore out this estimate, another statement being that rods
which sold for £50 a ton in 1921 fetched only £30 a ton in
1922.   In Warwickshire, rods which had fetched as much
as £60 or £70 during the war were said to be sold in 1922
at £20 a ton.

The result of the general uncertainty in the trade and the
sudden drops in prices between 1920 and 1923 was that
basket-makers became increasingly reluctant to buy the
crops of local growers, preferring to order only such rods as
they were certain of needing for immediate use, which could
more easily be obtained in sorted bundles from the dealers.
There has always been some element of risk in the buying
of a whole crop, and when prices fell so rapidly this was
greatly increased.   Thus the small grower found it more and
more difficult to dispose of his produce, and became more
unwilling, and at the same time, financially unable, to
employ the necessary labour on the cultivation of his rods.
These circumstances, of course, had an unfavourable effect
on the quality of the rods produced, and so, by this vicious
circle of cause and effect, the difficulty of selling them was
further increased.

Raw materials, other than willow, are used by many
basket-makers.   Of these materials the most important is
cane.   Basket-makers usually buy it from London firms of
importers or, in small quantities, from the firms who deal
in all varieties of material, as well as the tools and appliances
used by them.   Whole cane is used for very heavy work,
such as factory skeps and large fish baskets, and for
strengthening the edges of transport hampers and other
baskets which receive rough usage.   In its split or ' manufactured ' state it is used for seating chairs, for fancy baskets,
and for the best quality of furniture.   Much of this manufactured cane comes through France and Germany, but
since the war the plant required for splitting cane has been
installed by a firm near Leicester.   Four strips are split off
each rod, leaving the round centre, or pith, which is used
for making light baskets and cane furniture, whilst the split-
off strips are used for seating chairs.

Rush plait is sometimes woven into furniture or fancy
baskets, in conjunction with cane or osiers, for the purpose
of decoration.   The long strips of plait used to be made up

in England in different centres near the Avon and other
rivers in which the rushes grow,[1] but very little English
plait is now used, as it can be produced more cheaply abroad.
It is imported from Belgium and Holland. Great quantities
of it are used by the Nottinghamshire and Bridgwater firms,
and one of the latter had cutting rights over a certain reach
of the river Avon, whence they obtained rushes which were
plaited in their Bridgwater works, both for local use and
for sale to basket-makers in other districts. Straw plait,
imported from China, is also used in fancy baskets for
decorative purposes.

IV. *The Cultivation of Osiers and Preparation of the Rods for Market.*

Knowledge of the kinds of soil on which willows can be
grown with success and of the varieties of willow best suited
to any kind of soil is still incomplete, and there is room for
research in these matters. It has already been mentioned
that the kind of soil on which willows seem to thrive best
is a rich, well-watered heavy loam (as in the Trent Valley),
and that they have also been found to do well on dry, sandy
ground with a good top soil (as at Mawdesley), on poor loamy
clay and even on peat (as on Sedgemoor). Mr. Hutchinson
has stated that willows ' are generally grown on the low lands
bordering on streams. No other crop is as suitable to periodically flooded land, and in regard to economic husbandry this
is their right place.' [2] Growers in Gloucestershire find it
easy to obtain land along the banks of the Severn. It would
be extremely interesting to discover in this neighbourhood,
so much influenced by the tidal Severn, whether osiers can
be grown in brackish water, and what sort, if any, thrive
under such conditions, and which can endure the greatest
quantity of salt in the water. Another interesting subject of
research would be to discover if land that is now covered or
partially covered by the river at high tide or in flood time
could be raised in level by successive plantings of osiers and
eventually turned to more important uses. Very rich grazing
lands are now to be found in the neighbourhood of the Severn,
especially on the flat plain that stretches from Berkeley towards the river ; if these could be increased in area by some
such measure as the above, it would be to the future advan-

---

[1] See Chapter III. Rush, Sedge, and Reed Industries.
[2] ' Willow growing and Basket making ', *Journal of the Board of Agri-culture*, February 1916.

tage of the farmer, as well as to the present advantage of the willow-grower and basket-maker.

The same kind of land does not suit all varieties of willow. One of the greatest difficulties in willow-growing is to suit the variety to the land and, when planting willows for the first time, expert advice is essential if the crop is to have a good marketable value. A poor variety may do better on land that is suited to it than a good one on the same land if the soil is not appropriate. The effect of heavy soil on the willow is to give what the growers and basket-makers call ' nature '— toughness—of a sort that is ' kind ' or pliable. This is a valuable quality in basket rods. It is said that ' land that will bear fat beasts will bear good willows'. Willows are sometimes grown on sewage farms, though not always with success. Sewage willows are usually of inferior quality and do not ' buff ' to such a rich, even colour as others. Moreover, the cutting of sewage willows is not a pleasant task, and the corporation owning the farm usually tries to sell the rods as a standing crop to avoid the trouble of arranging for the cutting, peeling, and preparation for sale. If a common osier, which is naturally prone to florid growth, is planted on a sewage farm, the fatness of the land tends to ' blow it up ' and the rods will ' spelch ', or break at the edges, when worked, and thus are of little use to the basket-maker. A certain type of willow, however, has been discovered to be suitable to the conditions of the sewage farm, a variety known as *S. hippophaifolia*, which is believed to be a hybrid between *S. viminalis* and *S. triandra*, two of the species most in use for basket rods.[1]

Difference of soil has been known to change a variety to a great extent. One grower had Black Maul grown on high land, at Pavenham, and also on low land in the valley of the Nene. Both were ' buffed ' together, but the former came out a deep reddish colour and the latter a very pale buff. The variety known as Glibskins is said to grow crooked in a certain holt in Northamptonshire, whereas in other places it grows straight. Mr. Ellmore gives an instance of an American rod, Welch, which was entirely different from the English rod of the same name but which, when planted in England, could not be distinguished, after three years growth, from the English variety. A theory held in the Trent Valley to explain the relatively poor quality of Somerset willows is that the Somerset growers have not yet found the varieties really suited to their land.

[1] W. P. Ellmore, *The Cultivation of Osiers and Willows.*

The innumerable species within the genus *Salix* are a subject of great difference of opinion amongst botanists. From the industrial point of view they may be classed as those that grow to timber size and those whose habit of growth is low and bushy and whose shoots can be cut yearly for basket rods. The varieties used for baskets belong to three species, *S. viminalis*, or common osier, a soft willow, often known as a 'full top', *S. triandra*, or willow, a hard willow, known also as 'fine top', and *S. purpurea*, or bitter willow, also a hard rod. The distinction between willows and osiers is not generally observed, except by the more scientific growers.[1] Until the nineteenth century only *S. viminalis*, in some forty of its varieties but quite uncultivated, formed the staple basket-making material in England, but in the early part of that century attention was given to the cultivation of this species of willow. In a report written by T. Selby, of Otford, Kent, as early as 1800, the writer shows that he has been making experiments in the matter. William Scaling, of Basford (Notts.), about the middle of the nineteenth century, made many experiments and published pamphlets on the subject, and in Germany, J. A. Krabe, of Prummern, near Aachen, published his *Lehrbuch der nationalen Weideskultur* in 1886. The study of the cultivation of the willow, especially of the *Purpurea*, was given an impetus by the discovery by Leroux, in 1831, of the bitter principle in willow bark from which salicin is made. Quinine was at one time extracted from the liquor in which 'Dicky Meadowes', a variety of *Purpurea*, had been boiled. Both these natural products have now, however, been superseded by the coal-tar products.

Each of the three chief species of willow used for basket-making has its own characteristics from the basket-makers' and the growers' point of view. *Viminalis*, the osier, grows on poor ground better than *Triandra*, and thrives under dry conditions. It is used for coarse work of any sort and also for 'skeined' (pronounced 'skeened') work—that done with split rods. Longskin, the best kind of osier, is alternatively called Longskein, and is often skeined or split. *Triandra* requires good, heavy soil, and when grown on such land its 'nature' is like whipcord. It is used for chairbacks and all 'fitched' work (that done with two rods twisted together as they are woven), and, in fact, for any work that requires strength and fine quality. *Purpurea*, the most famous variety of which is Dicky Meadowes, is one of the few kinds

[1] Cf. note on p. 3.

of willow that will grow well in sandy soil. It is used for all kinds of fine work, such as the making of shopping and fancy baskets. Certain varieties, known as Kecks, are suitable for skeining. This species is said to have, at times, such a wonderful 'nature' that 'you could lace your boots with it'. It is very small in size and expensive to grow, as there is not much weight to the acre, but it always fetches high prices.

Basket-makers say that wild willows, as a rule, have no 'nature', or that, if by chance they have it, it is not 'kind'. One grower told of some willows which he had found growing wild on the west coast of Cumberland whose nature was of the 'kindest', and which strongly resembled a variety of Dicky Meadowes called White Bud. Although it is probable that these were escapes from some cultivated plot, it is obvious that the climate and soil must have suited them for them to maintain their quality without cultivation.

Since the art of cultivation of the willow has been carried to its highest pitch in the Trent Valley, a list of the kinds in common use there is given :

S. viminalis, the common osier : Longskin, Silverskin, Black, White, and Green Osier, Black top, Merrin or Yellow Osier, Kellum, Blob, and Black rod (a cross between a *Viminalis* and a *Triandra*, grown at Castle Donington).

S. triandra, the hard willow : Black Maul or Mole, Black German, Wissender or Newkind (also called Black Norfolk), White Dutch Newkind, Somerset Newkind, Stone Rod or Brown Spaniard, Golden Chelsea and other golden varieties, French willow, Spaniard, Hibbert (also called Glibskin or Wilkinson).

S. purpurea, the bitter willow : Dicky Meadowes—Red Bud, White Bud, and Blue Bud—Red Kecks and White Kecks, Scalings (also called Basfords or Mawdesleys).

In most districts of the Trent Valley the Black Maul or Black German holds the field in popularity, but growers near Gainsborough put their faith in the Wissender.

Sedgemoor, with its spongy peat subsoil and winter flooding, is not suitable for the finer varieties of willow, but the coarser sorts, known in this district as rods, as distinct from osiers, yield very heavy crops. Even on Sedgemoor improvement in the quality of the rods has been effected in recent years by the discarding of inferior sorts, and there is a tendency, increasing since the war, to plant on water meadows with a firm clay subsoil, on pasture not liable to flooding and even on arable land, rather than on the peaty moor. The favourite variety is Black Mole ; Champion and

Newkind are also found frequently, and Red Bud is said to be suitable. A grower and merchant, 80 per cent. of whose withies are Black Mole, named as the necessary kinds, in order of merit, Black Mole, Champion Rod (said to be another variety of Black Mole), Stone Osier, Mealy Top, and Old French.

The most famous variety grown in Lancashire is Dicky Meadowes. It is said to have been discovered by a certain Richard Meadowes who lived in Mawdesley. He brought some raspberry canes from abroad, and by planting the withies with which these were bound he produced this highly prized variety of bitter willow. Besides Dicky Meadowes, or Dicks, there are grown around Mawdesley Longskins, Purple Rods, Mawdesleys, and others.

Growers in other districts often do not distinguish one kind from another, and say either that they grow ' all kinds ' or that there is only one kind and that is the common osier. Certain varieties, however, are extensively grown and known by name in many counties. Of these Black Maul is the most popular, and is mentioned by almost every grower who knows any varieties by name. Worcestershire seems to be the only county in which willows are cultivated to any extent where this variety is not known ; here Black Spaniard takes its place, together with a kind called Black Sally. This latter seems to be merely a dialect name for a black willow of some sort, sally being, of course, the same word as sallow, which is a general term applied to willow or any soft wood.

In the districts where fruit pots are made—the counties of Gloucester, Worcester, Hereford, and Warwick—Clay Rods and Stone Rods are popular. The latter were also mentioned in Yorkshire. Other Warwickshire varieties are Gold Stone (also known in Gloucestershire) or Keck, and a kind known as Fast-Grower, which is said to be tall and coarse, with no ' nature '. Varieties described as Red, Brown, and Yellow Willows, and also Longskin, were found in Gloucestershire. Spaniards are grown in Yorkshire for scuttle making, and in the Fen Country where they are used in skeins for stitching straw skeps. Newkinds are used in Yorkshire and through-out the Fen Country, where they are distinguished as Black Newkinds and White Newkinds. Other sorts found in York-shire were Common Osiers, Brown Tops, Golden Osiers, Brownskin and Redskin and Black German. Other Fen Country varieties are, in addition to Black Maul, Red and Golden Maul, and Golden Willow, the last being used for tying celery. In Cambridgeshire, Brown Hollands, Glibskins, and Red Rods are also grown, and in a large holt near Peter-borough there were Brown Hollanders and French and Welsh willows. A variety known as Nottingham Osier was found in Northants, and here Dutch Osiers, which are light coloured and soft and fit close together when plaited, were planted especially for scuttle-making. In one small plot near Berwick, the owner of which showed great interest in the different varieties and their cultivation, Spaniards, Black Norfolks, Common Osiers, and a Golden variety are grown. Champion and Newkind were mentioned near Guildford, and Newkind again, Bent Willows and Yellow Willows at Rye. Yellow Osiers are grown in Cornwall.

The accommodating capacity of some varieties of willow to grow almost anywhere has given rise to the idea that no cultivation is necessary for this crop. Nevertheless the best growers have shown that no crop responds more readily to careful husbandry. The influence of the standard of cultivation of willows in any locality upon the basket-making industry of the neighbourhood, and vice versa, can be seen in the Bridgwater, Trent Valley, and Fen districts. In the Trent Valley, where the growing and preparation of willows is a fine art, the best basket work is done ; the Bridgwater industry is of a lower grade owing to the poorer quality of Sedgemoor withies, whilst, conversely, in districts such as the Fen Country, where the rougher kind of baskets for agricultural use or the packing of fruit are the chief product, the local standard of willow cultivation is on the whole a low one.

The preparation of the ground for a willow crop is of the utmost importance. Very deep ploughing or digging is necessary. Certain growers who have high standards of willow cultivation believe in using a steam plough once or twice over the land and a steam cultivator as many as eight times. Between the ploughing and the cultivating men and women go over the ground clearing away weeds. If a plough is not used, careful growers have the ground dug ' the full draw of the spade and half a draw below ' or two spits deep. In the Trent Valley the total cost of preparing the ground by means of steam tackle, together with labour for weeding, the cost of sets and of planting, the incidental expenses connected with hedging, ditching, and draining, and the cultivation during the first year had amounted to £100 an acre during the season 1920–1 in a case in which the greatest possible amount of care had been expended on every process. The preparation of the ground in a less ambitious manner, such as would probably be employed by a small grower, together with planting, could be carried out at this time at a total cost of from £40 to £60 per acre. In Somerset the total cost of preparing the ground and planting and keeping the beds clean during the first year was estimated in 1920 as about £48 5s. per acre, whilst before the war it could have been done for £9 15s. an acre. The cost of the sets was the largest item in the Somerset estimate, amounting to £25. In other districts much less care is usually given to the preparation of the land, at a correspondingly lower initial outlay counterbalanced by smaller returns on the crops.

The number of sets needed to plant an acre is from fifteen to twenty-four thousand, according to the method of planting. In districts where the cultivation of osiers is not very carefully studied the grower needing sets cuts them from his own holt. Even in the Trent Valley some growers use their own sets when they have a variety which has already done well on the land and do not want to risk a change. Other growers, however, believe that sets planted on the land from which they were cut will lose their vitality, or that one variety will exhaust the land if grown on it continuously, and therefore they obtain their sets from other growers. Some growers insist on sets cut from shoots of only a year's growth, others are content with those from two or three year olds. Several sets can be cut from one rod. In the Ely garths set-cutting was seen in progress in the early spring, side by side with the trimming of the rods. Certain rods were selected and sets were cut off their butt ends by means of a set cutter, a species of shears with one blade fixed on a stand and the other worked by means of a long handle. The sets, as they were cut, were piled up neatly between four sticks stuck in the ground. In Somerset the sets were cut thirteen inches in length. A good planter will push them into the earth so that it is unnecessary to go over the ground again to make the soil firm. He carries the sets in his left hand and pushes them in with the palm of his right hand, which is protected by a leather shield. His forefinger measures the height (three inches) of the piece left above ground. He can gauge the correct distance from set to set without measurement, but has a line to keep his ranks straight.

The distance between the sets in planting depends upon whether a horse hoe is afterwards to be used in the beds. In the Trent Valley the modern system is to put in the sets eighteen inches apart in either direction. This leaves room for a horse hoe to go both up and down the ranks and across them. More conservative growers leave twenty inches between the rows and nine inches between the plants and use a hand hoe, or if a horse hoe is used it only goes up and down the ranks.   In Somerset the usual method is to leave twenty-two inches between the ranks and fifteen inches from set to set.   Here the horse hoe is used between the ranks and seventeen thousand sets to the acre is the usual allowance. Some growers prefer to plant closely in order to make the rods grow straight, ' They pull each other up ', as one grower explained.   Moreover, the horse does a certain amount of damage to the crop and the hoe is apt to go too deep, with the result that the willows scab at the base.   On the other hand, the heads will grow more rods when there is greater space between them, and many growers consider that it is of little consequence if the rods are slightly bowed at the base during the first few years ;   when worked in a damp state, as they are by the basket-maker, the rods straighten out easily enough.   Stools planted wide apart may bear as many as twenty-five rods to a head, whereas when narrow planting is adopted six or seven to a head is more usual.   The harm done by the horse hoe is considered by the more advanced growers as slight compared with the saving of time and money effected.   In the districts where willows are not very carefully cultivated a horse hoe is seldom used.   On rough, uneven land it is not practicable, and when the willows are grown on very small or narrow strips of land, as is often the case alongside a stream, the waste of space on the ' headland ', necessitated by the use of the horse hoe, is a serious consideration.

There are many risks in connexion with planting.   For the first year the crop is very dependant upon the weather. Even in a season in which the old plants do well there may be losses among the young plants.   It is considered that, as a rule, no receipts from the maiden crop should be reckoned when estimating the possible profits from a new osier-bed. This crop may even be a source of expense in cases where the grower has to pay to have it carted away.   If the season is favourable it may produce three tons to the acre.   The Trent Valley grower already mentioned, who spent £100 per acre in the preparation and planting of a holt, sold the maiden crop at the rate of £100 per acre in 1921, but this was a very exceptional case.   The usual estimate is that, under normal conditions, receipts by the end of the third year should have repaid all expenditure.

Most Trent Valley growers consider that an osier-bed, to be kept in first-rate condition, should be hoed, either by hand or by a horse hoe, three times each year, in early spring and summer. Once the ground is neglected and weeds become established and their roots entangled with the willow roots, they can only be cut above the ground. All growers who take a keen interest in willow cultivation are emphatic on the question of weeding. As one of them said, ' No land will bear two crops and if it bears weeds it won't bear willows ', whilst another explained that ' the beds must be kept clean—clean like the back of your hand '.

The Lancashire method of keeping the beds clean is to use a ' double reefed ' plough early in the year ; this throws the earth over the stumps and it is later removed by hand. Later in the year, when the shoots are too high to allow of the use of machinery, men are employed, if necessary, to weed by hand. These beds, seen in June, looked particularly neat and clean. Somerset growers maintain that if the beds are hoed thoroughly during the first three years of their life all that is necessary thereafter is to cut down the weeds each year when the rods have grown. It is said here that when the withy beds are established the thick, tall growth of the rods is enough to keep down weeds. The dropping leaves of the willows supply all that is needed as regards manure. In other districts, where most of the rods are grown only for local use in rough work, some growers, particularly farmers whose osier crop is only a side line, do no more than clean the beds once a year. Few small growers, except in the Trent Valley area, do more than this, although some admit that their holts are not kept as clean as they should be. There are, however, several growers on a larger scale outside the Trent Valley who have quite a high standard of cultivation. One of them declared that ' beds *must* be wed at least three times a year'. The rapid fall in the prices of rods, the general uncertainty in the industry and the high cost of labour in the years following the war, rendered the owners of many beds unable or unwilling to continue to spend money on keeping them clean whilst they had no prospect of securing any adequate return for the outlay. Once a bed deteriorates seriously it costs almost as much to get it into good order as to plant afresh. Even before the war a grower who had taken over a neglected bed had expended £40 an acre to get it into good condition.

A weedy bed renders the willows more liable to blight by weakening the stocks. Blighted shoots branch out sideways and their value as rods is diminished. Spraying is the only remedy, but it is often neglected owing to the cost. Pollard willows, which are sometimes cultivated, especially for 'sticks' (the strong two or three year old rods used in furniture), are particularly liable to blight, and so are the withies grown on Sedgemoor.

The length of the life of a willow holt varies according to the variety grown, the suitability of the soil and the care given to the crop. A holt comes to full bearing capacity about the fourth year. On poor ground it may not last for more than ten years, but under good conditions twenty or thirty years of bearing may be expected, and in exceptional circumstances a holt has been known to produce good rods for forty years. In the Trent Valley this is the greatest length of time for which a holt is allowed to remain. At the end of this period, if not before, it is rooted up and the ground ploughed, dug, and manured to prepare it for a fresh planting of willows or some other crop. In Somerset it was said that beds might continue to yield heavy crops for as long as thirty years if poor roots are replaced by new ones from time to time. A Sedgemore grower, however, estimated the average life of a bed on peat as fourteen years. When the yield diminishes here the beds are let down to grass, the stumps being rooted up. The land is grazed for four or five years and is then ploughed up and other crops are grown. Some growers, who do not expend much care on their beds, let them down to grass after seven or eight years' growth and replant after another five years.

Growers in other districts, with the exception of those at Mawdesley and a few in different parts of the country who own large holts, seldom think of uprooting a whole bed and replanting. They merely remove old stumps from time to time, putting in very tall sets, about three feet high, just after the rods have been cut, so that the new shoot has the greater part of a year's growth on it before the older shoots grow up around it. A bed treated in this way will 'go on for ever', according to the rather indifferent standards of these growers.

The rods are cut with a hook, the near sides of two ranks being cut in one journey. A sharp upward movement, deft and quick, is needed, and the rods should be cut as close as possible to the stump. Good cutting is as important to osier stumps as good pruning is to fruit trees. A good cutter was once described as leaving the heads 'as neat as a Savoy cabbage'. In an osier-bed where the rods have always been carefully cut the stools are but little higher than the level of the ground. With bad cutting they grow taller and

SORTING OSIERS

STACKING BROWN RODS

taller, till they are sometimes a foot above the ground.
After very careless cutting the stools may have to be trimmed.
A story was told in Gloucestershire of a marshy osier-bed in
which, after the hunt had drawn it and passed on, a fox was
found snugly asleep on an osier stump. The fact that the
stump was tall and large enough to provide the fox with a
dry bed out of harm's way demonstrates the careless cutting
to which the osier-bed had been subjected.

The cut rods, if they are to be used brown, are by a careful grower trimmed before being tied up in bundles. A man
standing by the loosely piled, newly cut rods takes them up
one by one and slices the twigs off each with a hook. The
trimmed rods are made into bundles, each bundle being
bound by two withies, and stacked.

Rods as used by the basket-maker are either brown, white,
or buffed. The brown are simply stacked to dry with the
bark on, the white are those which have been peeled, and the
buff are those which have been boiled in their skins, and thus
stained a fine buff colour with the tannin from the bark, and
afterwards peeled. A great deal of buffing is done by Trent
Valley growers, and in this district cutting and buffing begins
in November and continues until April ; peeling white begins
when the buffing season is over. Nearly all the Mawdesley
osiers are buffed, and here the work begins in October. A
certain amount of buffing is also done in Somerset, but by
many firms here the rods are buffed in the summer, the work
beginning in July as soon as peeling white is over. Cutting,
however, begins in November, as in the Trent Valley,
except on certain beds which are liable to flooding, which
renders steady work impossible until after January. In
most other districts buffing is not carried out, all the rods
being sold brown or peeled white. When no buffing is done
cutting may not begin until the spring.

Unless special precautions are taken to preserve the rods
in the right condition they can only be peeled white during
about six weeks, between the beginning of April and the end
of June, whilst the sap is rising and the willows bursting into
leaf. The peeling period can be lengthened by several
different methods, which are described by Mr. Hutchinson.[1]
The methods he enumerates are : ' (1) Growing several
varieties which attain in succession to the best peeling condition, (2) Couching, which consists in placing the bundled
spring-cut rods in definite order forming heaps, (3) Pieing,

---

[1] H. P. Hutchinson, ' Willow Growing and Basket Making ', *Journal of
the Board of Agriculture.* February 1916.

in which the bundles are placed on the ground, one layer thick, heating being prevented by repeated watering and turning ' (Yorkshire growers added that it was important to stack the rods on some foundation to keep them clear of the earth. They cover the rods with peelings), ' and (4) Pitting, in which the rods, cut in March, are bundled and placed on end in ditches or in specially constructed pits through which water is induced to flow. Root, flower, and leaf development takes place, but secondary thickening is slow, so that peeling may be continued until July.' The last method is very frequently followed along the Severn and in the Ely district. In Somerset about four fifths of the rods which are to be peeled are pitted, only one fifth being stripped immediately they are cut. It saves labour to peel, or strip, at once, but this may necessitate hurried cutting which spoils the stocks. In Yorkshire the rods are often pied and may be kept in this way for three months. The labour necessary for either pitting or pieing adds greatly to the cost of the peeling process, and this is a deterrent to small growers who are often only able to peel as many rods as can be dealt with immediately they are cut.

If peeling is started too early the bark does not come clean off the butt ends of the rods. The process is a very old one. Xenophon, in his account of the Thirty Tyrants of Athens, tells of the exiled Greeks who had seized on the Piraeus making themselves shields of ' whitened osiers '. They had evidently discovered that whereas unpeeled rods hold moisture and rot quickly, the wet does not soak into the peeled rods. This is why farmers are often willing to pay the extra price for agricultural baskets made of peeled rods.

In peeling, the rods are drawn through a break, of which different patterns are in use. One kind consists of two strips of slightly curved steel screwed together at their lower ends so that their upper parts curve away from one another. The inner sides are faced with rounded pieces of iron. The break is fastened to a wooden bench and each rod is pressed down into it and drawn through, the spring of the steel being strong enough to squeeze the bark off. The slight outward curves of the pieces of steel form a neck widening towards the top so that the break fits any size of rod. Another type of break is formed of two S-shaped pieces of steel placed back to back to form a flask shape, the rods being drawn through the narrow neck at the top. Illustrations of several different types of break are given by Mr. Ellmore.[1]

[1] W. P. Ellmore, *The Cultivation of Osiers and Willows.*

TRIMMING AND TIEING BUNDLES

BUNDLES STANDING IN PIT

The buffing process is said not to have been known outside England until recently. Since the war it has been more widely adopted on the Continent, many Belgians having learnt the process when they were refugees in this country.

The Trent Valley method of buffing is to boil the rods for from two to five hours and leave them to cool overnight. They are peeled the next day by women, who stand around the tank picking out the still hot rods as they need them. The peelers wrap rags round their fingers to prevent soreness, and remove the bark by pulling the rods through their hands. In Somerset, much of the buffing is done by outworkers in their own homes, and this means that the rods must be boiled and then distributed to the strippers, who may live some distance away. Some firms do not have boilers of their own, but send the rods elsewhere to be boiled. Rods which have been allowed to cool and become partly dry before they are stripped are not so soft as those which are taken straight from the tanks, and breaks must therefore be used for the stripping. If the rods have become too dry they may be soaked again before stripping, but this has not quite the same effect as peeling them when still soft from boiling. The breaks, moreover, are apt to crack and injure the boiled rods, which have become brittle and tender. The Somerset method of buffing accounts to a great extent for the inferiority of Somerset rods, which have been described by Trent Valley growers, with picturesque exaggeration, as ' all smashed to ribbons by the breaks '. A certain amount of buffing in Somerset is carried out in stripping yards or sheds on the growers' premises, but even in these cases the rods are sometimes sent away to be boiled.

In the Trent Valley the yield from a holt is calculated by weight, but the weight of a given quantity of rods may vary considerably according to the relative proportions of pith and wood, and these depend upon the season. The quality of the rods also varies from year to year, even with the most careful cultivation. The crop one year may be suitable for peeling and selling as white rods and next year may only be fit to be sold as brown rods and may be no more than two thirds in weight of what it was the year before. ' Hullings ', rods of the smallest size, may weigh from twelve to fourteen pounds a bundle one year and only eight or nine pounds another year for a bundle of the same circumference. When little care is given to cultivation the variability is even greater. One estimate of the yield from holts in this district was that stools of three years' growth may bring seven tons to the acre ; another grower considered that eight tons to the acre from ten-year-old stools was a high figure. The weight of the crop, of course, depends on the variety of willow grown as well as on other circumstances. Two and a half tons to the acre is considered a good yield for Dicky Meadowes, a particularly small rod. The quantities of Somerset withies are always calculated in bolts instead of by weight, and as the amount of material which goes to a bolt is variable it is difficult to estimate the yield in tons per acre. The average yield in this district is estimated at about sixty bolts of white rods per acre the first year, a hundred and thirty the second, and from two hundred to three hundred bolts per acre from the third onwards. A large firm cultivating two hundred acres put the average yield at two hundred bolts per acre, whilst an expert grower reckoned to get a hundred and fifty bolts from his half-acre plot, probably by more intensive cultivation. These estimates are all calculated in peeled rods. About three tons of green rods make one ton when peeled, and about two hundred bolts of white rods go to the ton, so that the average yield of Somerset beds would seem to be from three to four and a half tons of green rods per acre in full bearing capacity, a low average when compared with the Trent Valley figures, but one which may be accounted for perhaps by the lower standard of cultivation in Somerset.

In Worcestershire the yield was estimated at from two thousand to three thousand bundles of green rods, from a ten to twelve acre holt—about two hundred and twenty-seven bundles per acre—but the weight of these bundles was not given. The yield from a certain two and a half acre holt had fallen from an average of eight hundred bundles before the war to two hundred bundles—and those of poor quality— in 1920, owing to lack of cultivation.

In Somerset it was estimated that before the war a man might, with the help of his family, work a five-acre withy bed, and the maximum return from the crop would be £260 in a year. In addition to the help which wife and children could give it would probably be necessary to hire labour for the cutting of the rods, and there is also the expense of carting to be considered. In a bad season the crop would not fetch so much, and blight, to which the Sedgemoor beds are peculiarly liable, might ruin a whole crop. During the war the return from withy beds worked by family labour was estimated at a maximum of £70 per acre. It was said that between 1914 and 1920 growers who employed labour might realize from £70 to £90 per acre net profit.

The rental of osier-beds in the Trent Valley is low compared with other districts and increased very little during or since the war. The usual rent in 1920 seemed to be from £2 to £3 an acre, as much as £4 or £5 an acre being heard of occasionally. Agricultural land in the same district lets at from £1 to £1 10s. an acre. Rents of osier-beds here apply chiefly to the small growers, for nearly every grower of importance owns his land.

In Somerset the rental was higher, averaging in 1920 about £6 an acre, but varying considerably according to the proximity of the bed to a good road or to the river. On Sedgemoor, when an osier plat is badly situated, large sums must be spent on the cartage of the bundles by boat along choked ditches or along muddy, spongy droves. Growers in this district are therefore willing to pay considerably higher rents for more conveniently situated beds. The *price* of land for osiers in this district ranged in 1920 from £70 to £130 per acre, and was enhanced by the competition for very small plots. Rates in Somerset were not assessed on the rents, for withy beds are not scheduled apart from pasture or meadow land. No new assessment had been made in the Bridgwater Union for about thirty years up to 1920, but the Langport Union had decided shortly before that to rate all withy beds on an average rental of £6, the former assessment being £2 10s.

The lowest rental for land under osiers was heard of in Sussex, where a bed near Lewes was rented at 35s. an acre in 1921. The grower, however, refrained from putting much labour into the bed lest the rent should be raised. In Gloucestershire rents range from £2 to £4 an acre, the higher rent being apparently exceptional. Poor marshy land is in this district easy to obtain at a low rental, but although it serves for the very indifferent osier cultivation which is common here, it would be of no use to an enterprising grower. In Worcestershire the rent charged ranged between £5 and £10 an acre, and most of the osiers were planted on marshy land unsuitable for other crops.

V. *Labour on Osier-beds.*

A certain amount of seasonal labour is always needed on osier-beds, but the variation in the number of men and women employed depends upon the scope and organization of the industry. Men are employed for the cultivation of the beds and the cutting of the rods, women for peeling both white and buffed rods and sometimes for additional help with weeding the beds. In districts where willow-growing is an old industry, as in the Trent Valley, or, even though new, a large and flourishing one concentrated in a small area, as in Somerset, seasonal labour is not difficult to get. The industry has its recognized place in local labour conditions. In the Trent Valley there are now a large number of men who have worked among willows throughout the whole of a long life and whose consequent skill and experience is valuable. In other districts, however, there is difficulty in obtaining additional labour when it is needed, and this is particularly the case with cutters. Cutting is skilled work ; when the osier-bed is owned by a basket-maker he or his men learn to cut the rods as part of their trade, or, again, when a big grower employs men in the industry all the year round he will always have a skilled cutter handy. But when casual labour is employed on the beds only for a few weeks in the year there is difficulty in getting sufficiently skilled cutters.

In the Trent Valley, where cutting is usually carried on continuously from November until the end of April, and where a great deal of labour is employed on the cleaning of the beds in spring and summer, the only slack time is from July to November, when the men can find work from farmers on the corn and potato harvests. On a twenty-acre holt only one man, a foreman, was employed all the year round, two or three more being kept at work, first on cutting and then on hoeing, from November to July.

In Somerset there is a slack season on some beds from November to January, because floods interrupt the work, but on other beds the cutting of rods to be used brown or to be buffed goes on from November to February, in February and March rods are cut and pitted to be peeled later, and the cutting of rods which are immediately peeled white continues through April and May. The beds are hoed and cleaned from April until the summer. August and September are the slackest months. On some large beds where as many as forty men were at work during the winter and spring only twenty were employed during these two months. There is always a certain amount of other work to be done. During the slack summer and early autumn months land can be prepared for planting. Even a small grower may need to root up some old stocks, or young sets which have failed, and replant. There is also the sorting of prepared rods, which, on large holts, may go on all through the year. In Worcestershire three men were employed during three months of the year in the cultivation of a sixteen-acre osier-bed and the cutting of the rods. The peeling is done by additional female

labour. The Somerset estimate of one man to five acres
tallies with this. On the other hand, if, for example, the
whole of a thirty-acre holt is to be cut within a few weeks for
peeling white, fifteen men may be needed.

Cutters are usually paid by piece rates, but some Somerset
employers object to this system because it may lead to hasty
and careless work, which injures the stumps and seriously
detracts from the value of the bed. They therefore pay their
cutters by time rates. Hoeing, weeding, and planting are
paid for by the acre, the rates varying according to the
condition of the beds. Most of the workers in this district
also rent beds which they work themselves, and are therefore
not entirely dependent on their earnings.

The Trent Valley employers who were paying relatively
high wages had few labour troubles, except in so far as they
suffered from the general scarcity of men during the war. In
the Gainsborough district, however, the absence of the Irish
labourers had caused acute difficulty, which had led one
grower to root up his willows and abandon his business.
Before the war the Irishmen came over in April and were
employed as cutters by growers who were peeling white
during April, May, and June. After June the Irishmen
worked for the farmers during the corn and potato harvests
and returned to Ireland for the winter. They were intelligent
and quickly trained, they became proficient cutters in a few
days and worked well. Being accustomed to rough conditions they were satisfied with such lodging as was available.

In Yorkshire the piece rate for cutting enabled a man to
earn from 9s. to 11s. a day in 1922. When a particularly small
variety of rod was being cut, day rates were paid, but the
grower declared that a piece of work which was done for
10s. by piece rates would cost him 14s. on day rates. In this
district, where the osier industry was small and relatively
unimportant, cutters were difficult to find. In Warwickshire
in 1923 6s. a day could be earned on cutting. In the Fen
Country cutting and tying were paid for by piece rates at
so much per bolt, the rate having risen to 1s. a bolt during
the war and fallen again to 3d. a bolt in 1923. A small grower
in this district sometimes contracted with a man to cut the
whole crop for a certain sum, and in the early months of 1923
the cutter's price of £5 for cutting a certain holt was said
to be equivalent to a wage of 35s. a week, and was considered
by the grower to be more than he could afford to pay.

In the Trent Valley women, helped by boys and girls, are
employed on peeling buffed rods throughout the winter until

April, and after that on peeling white for some weeks, but in many districts they are only needed for a few weeks in the spring during which the latter process is carried on. In Somerset they are employed on peeling white from April to July and after that on buffing during the summer months. Other Somerset firms, however, have buffing done in March and April. The women employed for buffing in the Trent Valley are of a rough and hardy type and many of them engage in other seasonal agricultural work. Although buffing is hot and dirty work it is done under shelter, a condition much appreciated in agricultural work in winter, and it is said to be healthy, the boiled rods giving out a pleasant acrid smell of tannin. The Somerset withy-stripping yards have a bad reputation, but this seems to be due to past rather than to present conditions. This is perhaps the reason for the development of the outwork system here, it being thought more desirable for young girls to work in their own homes. Here the greater part of the stripping is done by girls who start the work on leaving school and go into domestic service later. The peeling of white rods, as carried on in the Trent Valley in spring, may be compared to fruit-picking in other districts. The work is undertaken as a sort of annual outing, combining pleasure and profit. The social status of the strippers, as of all women workers in agriculture, is generally considered as below that of domestic servants. The work naturally tends to attract the hardier type of woman because of the exposure to weather and the hard wear on clothes. The more domesticated village girls naturally seek indoor work as servants rather than work in the fields and stripping yards. The spring peeling, however, is often done by married women who do not go out to work at all at other times of the year. The conditions suit them, as they can come and go when they please, although in the Trent Valley the hours are nominally from nine to four. They often bring their children, even the babies in prams, and all who are old enough help in the work. In districts where the osier industry is small and scattered and has not been long established there is often some difficulty in getting enough labour for stripping.

A grower with a holt of thirty acres who peels all his crop white will need thirty-five women for peeling during April, May, and June, although, if pitting or pieing is resorted to, the peeling period may be prolonged well into August, and fewer will be needed, but more men will be required to carry out the pitting or pieing process. An owner of twelve acres

PEELING OSIERS

PEELING OSIERS

PEELED OSIERS WHITENING IN
THE SUN

employed nine or ten women for eight weeks to peel the whole of his crop. A grower owning a very small holt, of only about four acres, employs four women on buffing throughout the winter and twelve for peeling white from April to June. Another grower had between four and five tons of rods (probably the crop from an acre or less), peeled by six women in six weeks. Another had from three to five women working for eleven weeks to peel eight tons. The time taken to peel varies considerably according to the size and quality of the rods, and the women work very irregularly, some of them only doing a very few hours each day. These figures show that even the smallest grower, if he peels his rods white, needs to employ several additional workers for a short season.

VI. Processes, Tools, and Labour in the Basket-making Industry.

The basket-maker's plant and workshop are of the simplest. He requires only a small shed with a dry floor and a normal supply of light and air. A tank is needed in which to soak the willows before use, and if he is to buff the rods himself he requires a boiler, but this would hardly be included in the equipment of the small-scale rural maker. If he is to buy standing crops of willows he will need several breaks for peeling, and these can be fastened to posts or to a bench in the yard. Brown rods can be stacked out of doors under a good thatch, but white and buff must be stored in a dry shed. Again, his method of buying material will affect the question of how much storage room is needed. Since the work is sedentary the workshop needs to be well warmed in the winter, and the heat of the stove brings out the peculiar acrid smell of the damp willows which is a pleasant characteristic of the basket-maker's surroundings. He sits on a sloping plank raised on a block at one end. His tools are few, consisting of one or two knives for cutting the rods and for trimming the basket by slicing off the rough ends, a triangular piece of iron to beat the work closely together, shears, and a device for straightening the sticks. Blocks for shaping the baskets, which are built up round them, are sometimes used when the labour of semi-skilled girls is employed, as on barrel-shaped shopping baskets and other kinds.

Willow branches of two or three years' growth are known as sticks, the others are rods. Sticks are used for the frame-work of heavy baskets or furniture. Some of the lighter kinds of basketry are woven with skeins, which are split rods. To split a rod into skeins a cleaver is used. This is a small implement cut out of box wood. It has three or four flanges, cut very fine and polished smoothly. It is held in the hand and pressed against the top of the rod which is thus split longitudinally into three or four parts. The cleaver is pressed down the whole length of the rod, dividing it into strips from end to end. After splitting, the skeins have to be drawn through a kind of spokeshave to make them more regular in shape and pliant.

The ' strokes ' most generally used in basketry are slewing, randing, and fitching. Slewing is working with two or three rods together, Randing the weaving of one rod singly, and Fitching is the twisting of two rods tightly under one another as they are woven in and out of the uprights. Fitching is used for ' skeleton ' or open work, such as poultry baskets. It is distinguished as ' eye work ' because the spacing needs to be accurately judged by the eye. It is said that blind men are unable to make fitched baskets for this reason. In making hampers and other large kinds the blind use an iron framework, placed inside the basket, as a guide to the shape.

The workers in the basket-making industry comprise men and women, boys and girls, but in the rural firms men are in the majority, all types of agricultural basketry being comparatively hard and heavy work, less suited to women than the making of baskets for domestic use.

Women are employed by the Bridgwater wicker-furniture makers, in the Trent Valley by firms which make furniture and fancy baskets, and in a few other workshops in different parts of the country where bicycle or shopping baskets are made, although this work is also done by men. Work with cane is particularly suitable for women, because the cane can be *pulled* into place, whereas the less pliant willow rods must be *put* into position, a process which requires both strength and skill. Women can also work well with willow skeins, as these thin slips are more easily manipulated than the whole rods. Probably a great many of the fancy baskets which come in such numbers to England from abroad are produced by the semi-skilled labour of girls, who quickly become competent to make one particular kind of basket, or even one part only of a basket, but have no experience in other branches of the industry. A certain English firm has found that, by employing a number of girls who have just left school on the light and easy task of making little work-baskets, under the supervision of a skilled forewoman, it is possible to compete with Germany in this type of work. In Suffolk a girl of sixteen was seen at work on agricultural baskets, which she seemed able to make as quickly and as well as most men. Her employer stated that he himself could make eight 'peck-cobs' a day, working from 8 a.m. to 5 p.m., but that he is an exceptionally quick worker ; the girl makes six of the same baskets in a day, and he declared that one of the recently trained ex-service men would only make two or three. It is, however, quite unusual to find girls or women employed by the makers in villages or small towns who supply local needs, except that sometimes a basket-maker's wife or daughter may do the rush and cane seating of chairs which are brought to him for repair.

Boys are largely employed in Bridgwater on the same kind of work as that done by women here and elsewhere. They do the ' filling in ' work with rush or cane on stick chairs, men having nailed the frame together, and they also make the seats of fitched chairs.

Basket-making is, from its nature, especially suited as a craft for the blind and otherwise disabled, being mainly a sedentary occupation and the material manipulated by the hands, with the use of few tools and those of the simplest. For long it has been more frequently practised by the blind than any other craft ; some of the workers in small rural firms are deaf and dumb or partly crippled, and large numbers of men blinded or otherwise disabled in the war have been trained in this industry.

Blind workers, other than ex-service men, are attached to the various County Associations for the Blind, receiving four or five years' training in the workrooms of the Associations, and afterwards either returning to their native town or village and setting up in business there independently, or continuing to work at the centre. Even in the former case, when they become home workers, the Association is partly responsible for the sale of their work, and it assists to main-tain the standard by means of visiting inspectors. The blind can do certain kinds of basketry as well as the sighted, but can never work quite so quickly, and must therefore have their earnings supplemented in some way ; the home workers receive a Government Grant under a scheme of the Ministry of Health. The blind workers do chair-caning and make the smaller kinds of baskets and sometimes larger ones ; in Yorkshire they make the big, heavy skeps for use in the textile factories. In Lincolnshire they make potato baskets, and butcher, butter, and market baskets. They cannot do furniture work very satisfactorily.

The St. Dunstan's men and other ex-service trainees receive, as a rule, a much shorter training than the ordinary basket-maker or the blind man attached to the County Association. The training of the former in basketry may extend only over a year or even for a shorter time. It is said that the St. Dunstan's man is generally more intelligent and able than the man who has been blind from birth through disease, which may have impaired his other faculties. But he does not at once develop the very sensitive touch which is a characteristic of those blind from birth, and his hands, unused to the more delicate kinds of manual work, have lost their suppleness. The ex-service men, being in receipt of pensions, only do basket-work as a supplementary livelihood, and sometimes do not practise it very seriously. Some, however, become very skilled and obtain employment in ordinary firms, one man, for instance, having been taken on by a firm which makes luncheon hampers for the railway companies. Legless men can do certain kinds of square work at a table ; others crippled in the legs can work at the plank in the ordinary way. Several of the trainees have since set up in business independently, but many others have not found basket-making sufficiently profitable and have given it up.

When the training of these men began, the basket-making industry was in a flourishing condition, and prospects seemed good, but in the present precarious and uncertain state of the industry the presence of this new class of workers tends to complicate the situation, and the fact that some of them are insufficiently trained and, even though skilled in one type of work, are unable to turn to another if a change in the market necessitates this, makes their position uncertain.

During the war the ordinary standards of training for able-bodied men seem to have deteriorated, owing to the increased demand for labour and the fact that it was easy for a boy to earn good wages by becoming skilled in one branch of work and practising that only. In Bridgwater the system of employing a quantity of juvenile labour without proper apprenticeship became very prevalent during the war. The boys were paid at a time-rate, the man responsible for their instruction taking the piece-rates for their work. In this way the desire of the boys to concentrate only on one sort of work, and thus become the more quickly skilled in it and able to earn good wages at piece rates, was encouraged by the teacher, who benefited by the greater amount of work they produced while under his charge. The result of this method will be to glut the labour market with an excessive number of semi-skilled men and will tend to lower the standard. The best firms, however, deprecate this system of training and pay the teachers by time-rates.

The necessary period of training is variously estimated at from three to five years. The complete training period before the war was five years, and in the Trent Valley it is still considered that a man cannot obtain skill in every branch of work in less than this time. Women on cane work need three or four years' training. The period devoted to training, however, depends entirely on the individual agreement made between employer and apprentice, as there are no trade regulations on the matter. An insufficient training sometimes leads to a man being deprived of his livelihood in middle age through a sudden change in the demand, which closes to him the market he has always supplied and leaves him unable, through the incompleteness of his knowledge of the craft and his inadaptability, to find a fresh opening. The general character of the English industry has changed considerably in the last thirty years, the manufacture of cane and wicker furniture increasing whilst the making of the smaller and lighter kinds of baskets is on the decline.

Outworkers are not generally employed in the basket industry, but they are numerous in the Bridgwater district, where the fact of their employment is said partly to account for the low standard of work. Technically they are not out-workers under a contract of service, for they buy material from the firm for which they work and sell their products back to it, thus avoiding all factory regulations as to hours of work, rates of wages, &c. It is stated that the firms who employ these home-workers are thus enabled to under-sell the Trent Valley makers of similar articles by exploiting this inferior labour. In this connexion it is interesting to note that the Dutch fruit baskets are said to be produced chiefly by family labour, employed, as here, by large firms who often grow osiers, sell the rods to the home-workers, and buy back the finished baskets. The poor wages and low standard of living among these Dutch basket-makers are said to account for the cheapness of their products.

In the Trent Valley and elsewhere an economy of labour is often effected by alternating work on the plank with work in the osier-beds, since the demands for labour on the latter arise only at certain seasons of the year. This system is found to be a convenient one by single-handed rural makers when business is slack, but in normal times the journeyman dislikes it because change of occupation causes the worker to lose pace.

For agricultural baskets the demand is seasonal, and many firms have for long been accustomed to employ additional labour during certain months of the year. For 'potato-pickers' the demand begins in October and may continue into December; feeding baskets of all kinds are chiefly needed during the winter, but the sale for these is, in any case, a comparatively small one; the greatest seasonal demand is for the baskets for fruit and market-garden produce, which, for a few sorts, begins in the early spring, and is at its height from June to September. The baskets are needed, of course, a little before the crop is actually ready for harvesting, and makers of fruit sieves say that orders generally begin to come in with the new year, so that their only slack time would be the autumn months and, if they made potato-pickers, these would keep them busy perhaps until November. The unsettled conditions of recent years have made the salesmen reluctant to place orders for baskets until the last moment, because of the ever existent possibility of a fall in prices, as well as the uncertain state of the fruit and vegetable market. It is also said that buyers wait to see what quantities of foreign baskets will be put upon the market and at what prices. The English makers are not, for the most part, very large or wealthy firms, and they cannot afford to make baskets for stock throughout the winter on the chance of there being a sale for them. If great numbers of baskets are accumulated storage becomes a problem, and if any are left on the maker's hands at the end of the season this has, during recent years, involved a serious loss for him, for the prices have fallen year after year and the selling price of a basket in, for example, 1923 often barely covered the cost of the material and the making of it in 1922.

There have always been a certain number of journeymen 'on the roads', who knew in which district they could be sure of work at certain seasons; a certain Gloucester firm employs as many as fifty additional men on pot-making for a few months in the summer; but the chance of employment for these travelling men is becoming more uncertain, conditions seeming to tend towards the employment of extra hands only for very short periods. It is said that the makers of foreign baskets are large firms who can afford to make

for stock, and launch the baskets on the English market in
great quantities at the moment when they are required.
English makers can obtain extra hands easily enough when
they require them, and this fact may cause them to dismiss
their workers more readily when times are bad, but trade
fluctuations and irregular work tend to lower the standard
and are therefore unfortunate in their effects upon the craft
as well as for the workers. Many employers have been heard
of, on the other hand, who have kept on their regular employees even when trade was so bad that they could hardly
make any profit on their work.

There is a very marked scarcity of apprentices or learners
in the trade, and even men under about thirty-five are rare.
In the whole of South Cornwall the investigator found, in
1921, only one boy learning the craft and one young basket-
maker. The explanation given was that the work done in
this district now is of a peculiarly heavy kind and therefore
unsuited to boys ; until about thirty years ago more varied
work was done here and boys and women were employed ;
at present the chief output of the South Cornwall basket-
makers consists of agricultural baskets of coarse workmanship for local use. But there are other districts where little
is made but baskets of this type, and where this has been the
case for a very long time, yet the present makers undoubtedly
learnt the work by serving an apprenticeship in their boy-
hood. The fact is that there is a scarcity of apprentices
to the basket industry for the same reasons which account
for the similar state of affairs in other rural industries all over
the country. In Yorkshire there was found, in 1922, only
one apprentice among twenty firms ; in the whole of Lincolnshire there were only two or three. In the Trent Valley,
where the industry is carried out on a larger scale, there
are a good many young men employed and quite a number
of apprentices. In one large firm there were actually a
dozen of the latter in 1921.

The general opinion amongst small rural firms seems to be
that wages were higher in 1922 and 1923 than the industry
could bear, but the amount earned by journeymen basket-
makers at that time was certainly not one on which they
could lead a life of excessive luxury. The few masters who
reported that the industry was, as far as they were concerned,
in a flourishing condition were generally men working alone,
without employees or helped only by their sons and daughters.
Owing to the depressed condition of agriculture at the time
farmers would either do without a basket or use some cheap

substitute, unless the price could be brought down to lower levels, and these cut prices caused many small rural makers to find that they could really make something more approaching a decent livelihood by working long hours unaided than by employing a man.

The rise in wages has been summed up as 30 per cent. at the beginning of the war, with a further 90 per cent. later, and a subsequent fall of from 30 to 40 per cent. In some cases the temporary rise was greater ; for example, the rate for making fruit pots was 7½d. before the war and 1s. 9d. in 1921, a rise of nearly 200 per cent. It is generally agreed that the rates before the war were lower than should have been current in a skilled trade, although they had improved considerably in the ten years before 1914, and old men who remember the appallingly long hours and sweated labour of an earlier period often have nothing but condemnation for the present conditions, which they describe as ' slacking ' and ' easy money '.

Basket-making is paid almost entirely by piece-rates, and there seem to be great variations in the earnings, apart from those dependent on the individual skill and speed of each worker. The rates current in some districts are those fixed by the Cane and Willow Workers' Associations and the Basket-Maker's Union, but in certain areas these organizations are very little in evidence. During the war certain groups of makers left the Association because they considered that the rates fixed, whilst perhaps suitable for the London area, were too high for an agricultural district ; in general the small country firms seem to be very weakly represented in the Association, and perhaps the special conditions of their work are hardly taken into account in deciding on the rates to be paid. Thus, the rates paid in any district probably depend chiefly on general usage and local demands for labour. Districts which were particularly notable in 1923 as paying rates below those fixed by the Association were Ormskirk, Selby, and the west of England.

In Ormskirk the earnings of a journeyman were said to average 36s. a week for 48 hours in 1923. In Worcestershire, at the same time, pots were made at 1s. a piece, thirty-six pots a week being an average output ; that is to say, the earnings would be the same as in Ormskirk. At this time the Union rate for pots was 1s. 2d. apiece, but in districts where this rate was in force hardly any employers could obtain orders for pots made on this basis of cost. Thus, although theoretically pot-makers in the suburbs of Birming-

ham were earning 42s. a week, actually very few were
earning anything at all, whilst in Worcestershire quite a
number, although less than before the war, were earning 36s.
weekly, and even so the profit of the employers was said to be
less than 20 per cent. Fen Country makers declare that
wages in Norfolk are below the rates in other districts and
the work is poorer ; thus, the Norfolk firms can produce
potato pickers at prices which can compete with those of the
imported Belgian baskets. The material used is locally
grown and of the roughest kind, and the makers are said to
put in a quarter of an hour less work on each basket than is
the case in the Fen Country. In the latter district the
maker ' opens ' the bottom of the basket, that is to say he
spreads out the bottom stakes at each end and inserts three
extra stakes. These bye-stakes are not used in the Norfolk
basket.

In 1923 it was estimated that a rural maker working on his
own, chiefly on agricultural baskets, would make on an
average £2 5s. a week, but probably many make less. A
man making egg-baskets, which he sold at 1s. each, said that
his output was from ten to twelve a day, but he was a slow
worker. A good man might make from fifteen to eighteen.
Thus, the maximum output of the latter would be to the
value of £5 8s. weekly. Twenty per cent. of this is only
£1 1s. 7d. which would represent the basket-maker's total
profit.

Pre-war earnings in the Bridgwater district averaged from
25s. to 30s. a week. In Lincolnshire, some time before the
war, potato pickers were made for 3s. 6d. a dozen ; the time
required for making a dozen would be twelve hours at least,
so that the earnings for a 54-hour week would be 15s. 9d.
This kind of work is perhaps the lowest paid of all. In Bedfordshire the pre-war rate for making flats was 10d. apiece,
and four could be made in a day of from 7 a.m. to 8 p.m.,
which would give the maker the sum of £1 for about sixty-six
hours' work.

During the war, when wages were at their highest, 1s. 2d.
was paid for making a potato picker, so that a man might
earn £3 15s. 10d. for a fifty-four hour week. He sunned
himself in the warmth of this amazing prosperity for a year
or two longer. In 1920 he received, in Bedfordshire, 2s 6d.
for making a flat, and he might turn out four of these in a day
of about eleven hours. Thus, he could earn £3 in a sixty-six
hour week. In South Cornwall, in 1920, the average earnings
on agricultural baskets were 1s. an hour ; younger men might

earn more, but hardly any of them were to be found among
the ranks of the basket-makers. A forty-eight hour week was
usually worked, with a half day on Saturday, but no regular
times were kept to, and no overtime rates were paid. 1s.
apiece was paid for making potato hampers and 2s. for
broccoli crates. It was said that twenty-seven to thirty of the
latter could be made in a week, which would represent a
wage of from 54s. to 60s. for this particularly heavy and
tiring work.

In the larger scale industries higher wages were earned.
In Bridgwater the average rate for a skilled worker was
1s. 5d. an hour, which was 1d. less than the Dockers' Union's
contemporary rate for labourers, but some of the most
expert workers were said to earn £3 and £4 a week and a few
even as much as £5 and £6. Particulars as to rates given
by one of the wicker-furniture firms in this district were
as follows : ' The hours generally worked are fifty-four per
week. 75 per cent. of the work is paid by piece rates, these
on the best work, i. e. cane chairs, being equivalent to
a time rate of 1s. 8½d. an hour. Piece-work rates on general
production rather exceed this average.' Women were said
to be earning approximately Trade Board rates, but the
earnings of those employed in family work were not estimated.

In the Trent Valley district, where labour was still scarce
in 1920, earnings were also comparatively high. In Derby,
in the autumn of 1920, the making of wine-hampers, which
is of the more skilled order of basketry, was paid at the rate
of 3s. 6d. each ; two could be made in a day, and some men
even made three, but others only one. 105 per cent. bonus
was paid, so that the daily wage of an average worker
would be over 14s. A large firm in Loughborough was paying
£3 to £4 a week for a good man on general work. In Leicester
£4 was said to be the maximum for forty-eight hours on
general work.

By 1922 wages had fallen considerably. In April of that
year pot makers in Worcestershire were earning in some cases
only at the rate of 10d. an hour, the rate for pots having
fallen to 1s. 4½d. each, which was reduced soon afterwards to
1s. 3½d. In Lincolnshire, in the autumn of 1922, the earnings
averaged from 1s to 1s. 6d. an hour, but the higher rates were
only paid by the few larger firms doing the finer kinds of
work. The most skilled men employed by one of these firms
on furniture work of the best quality received £3 for a forty-
hour week. Agricultural basket-work was more poorly paid ;
the rate for making potato pickers was 9s. a dozen, represent-

ing a minimum of twelve hours' work, so that for a week of fifty-four hours the wage would be 40*s*. 6*d*. In some parts of the East Midlands potato pickers were made for as little as 5*d*. each for a smaller size. Twelve in a day was said to be the maximum output of these ; an old man, who was a slow worker, made one in an hour : for a week of six full days the earnings of a good worker would be 30*s*. The rate for making flats was from 2*s*. 6*d*. to 2*s*. 7½*d*. each, and at the rate of output quoted by another maker—four in an eleven-hour day—the journeyman could earn a maximum amount of 15*s*. 9*d*. in a day of this length.

In 1923 the basket-makers of Warwickshire could earn on agricultural baskets not more than a labourer's wage if they worked a labourer's hours. In cases where the rods were bought from local beds, which frequently happened, they were bundled up roughly, unsorted, and untrimmed. An hour or so at the beginning of each day's work must be spent in preparing the material. This is particularly the case where rough material is used. For example, half an hour must be spent in preparing the material for the Quarter-cran, the big basket used for measuring fish in East Anglia, whereas the time spent on making the whole basket is only 1½ hours. The time worked by pot makers employed in Warwickshire was usually from 7.30 a.m. to 7 p.m., with 1½ hours off for meals, and six or seven pots would be made in a day. The rate was 1*s*. a pot, so that from 36*s*. to 42*s*. could be earned in a week consisting of six ten-hour days. The earnings for a forty-eight hour week would average only 31*s*. 2½*d*. It must be borne in mind that basket-making is a skilled craft, to become proficient in which a lad must spend from four to five years in apprenticeship, during which time he can earn very little and will probably waste a quantity of material by making baskets which will be unsaleable owing to their faulty shape. Also, on agricultural basket work, which is the lowest paid, there are always slack seasons with little or no work, and the earnings given above have always been reckoned on weeks of full time.

VII. *Kinds of Baskets*.

The following descriptive list includes the kinds of work chiefly produced by English rural basket-makers. It is compiled mainly from the information given by basket-makers in the East Midland counties and Lincolnshire, but is probably fairly representative of other areas. Varieties peculiar to special districts are listed separately.

§ 1. *Agricultural Baskets*

Potato Pickers are small baskets, round or oval, with a handle. The size varies in different districts, but is such as can be conveniently carried, when filled with potatoes, by the women who are employed to pick up the crop as it is turned up by the plough. On very heavy land the Pickers need to be smaller, as a good deal of earth clings to the potatoes. Some farmers have them specially made with an iron grid at the bottom through which the dirt sifts.

Potato Hampers are rough, square, open baskets, about 2 ft. high, with a hole near the top at each end by which they can be gripped. The potatoes are emptied out of the Pickers into the Hampers, in which they are carried to the pies.

Potato Skeps or *Skips* are used in place of the hampers in the Fen Country ; they are also known as bushel or half-hundredweight skeps. They are round or oval splayed-out white baskets, with handles for carrying. (For Potato Hampers see also under Transport Baskets.)

Sack Fillers, known also as Nancies, Bunks, or Sack Holders, are splayed-out baskets, generally brown, without bottoms. A Sack Filler holds four stone of potatoes and is used for filling the eight-stone sacks. The basket is placed in the bottom of the sack and filled, then lifted up so that the potatoes run through, placed on the top of them and filled again. This is called ' sacking up twice ', and the method serves to measure the potatoes put into the sack and also saves the labour of a woman who would otherwise have the cold task in the open field on a November day of holding the sack open while the potatoes are poured in.

Baskets for Cattle feeding. Various types of basket are used for feeding roots to cattle. Some farmers may prefer the ordinary hamper shape, but a kind more often used is the small *Feeder*, an oval open basket of splayed-out shape. Another kind used for winter feeding, for both roots and chaff, is a kind known variously as the *Chaff Cob*, *Chaff Skep* or *Chaff Basket*, *Feeding Skep* or *Field Scuttle* ; it is a very big round basket, of rough workmanship.

Scuttles, often distinguished from the above-mentioned kinds as *Wood Scuttles*, are a kind much valued by farmers. Makers of these baskets are now very few because the work is difficult and particularly onerous. Scuttle-making is not learned in the course of an ordinary apprenticeship, an extra year being served if a man wishes to become proficient in this particular craft, which is known in the trade as ' wood work '

AGRICULTURAL BASKETS

PIGEON BASKET

because strips, or ' spelks ', of ash wood are used in place of stakes. The ash must be rived with a knife and used green. If the spelks be sawn instead of rived with a knife they will break, being cut against the grain. Ulleskelf in Yorkshire was once the centre of a thriving scuttle industry and the basket-makers bought considerable quantities of standing ash for the purpose. Nowadays a tree or two bought now and then from a dealer in underwood is sufficient to supply each of the few makers who still do this work.

Scuttles are made in several sizes, the largest holding four bushels. They are round or oval in shape, splayed outwards from a small base, and sometimes bound round the rim with wire and strengthened at the bottom with two pieces of hoop iron. For a large scuttle four ash spelks, each 40 inches long, are used. These are laid on the floor, crossing one another, and the scuttle-maker takes off one boot and holds the spelks in place with his stockinged foot. He must then lean over his foot as he fills in the spelks with willow rods ; in fact, as one old man said, ' You must nigh stand on your head to make a scuttle '. Another man described how, after a scuttle-maker had been working for some time there could be seen a dark ring around him on the wooden floor, where the sweat dripped from his forehead as he bent over the work and turned from side to side, weaving the willows in and out of the ash spelks. Yet another old scuttle-maker remarked pathetically that he could never enjoy his dinner except on a Sunday. It is hardly surprising that young men are not eager to learn scuttle-making.

Some of the few who are skilled in this craft will make scuttles for their regular customers but for no one else. There are one or two makers each in Northants, the Holland division of Lincolnshire, and Yorkshire, and there are said to be some in Berkshire. They supply chiefly local customers, but some also make for a big dealer in baskets. A Yorkshire man estimated his output as twenty to thirty dozen yearly. Some basket-makers will not take the trouble to make scuttles themselves, but will obtain them from other makers for those of their customers who insist on having them.

Scuttle-making used to be poorly paid when many people made them and the competition tended to keep down the prices. The selling price of a scuttle was at one time only 9d. or 10d., but nowadays it is said that ' a farmer will run three or four miles to get hold of a good scuttle ', and they are sold at prices ranging between 3s 6d. and 5s., according to size, or at 50s. for a dozen of assorted sizes. It is said that a scuttle will stand rough usage for three years, and can then be re-bottomed, and takes on a fresh lease of life. The making of scuttles would therefore probably continue to be a flourishing and profitable industry if some method could be found of lightening the labour.

Another variety is the *Corn-scuttle*, similar to the above, but of oval shape, with a lip at each end and handles at the sides. It is used for pouring corn into sacks.

Seed-scuttles are used in market-gardening districts for sowing by hand. They are wood-scuttles of oval shape, with a wooden peg sticking up from the middle of one side and two handles on the other side. The sower holds the basket of seed under his arm, grasping the peg with his left hand, whilst a strap running through the handles and over his shoulder helps to support the weight.

Coal-scuttles are made at Sutton-on-Trent and are used in the docks for lading ships with coal. They hold one hundred-weight of coal and the dockers carry them on their shoulders. They are made with elm instead of ash spelks.

Stable Sieves, known as *Baiting Sieves* in East Anglia, are used for feeding chaff to horses. They are made of skeins— thin slips of willow rods, woven in an open mesh, surrounded by a wooden rim. The rims are not made by the basket-makers, but are obtained from dealers in appliances and materials for basketry. The dust from the chaff sifts away through the mesh of the sieve, which may be made of split cane instead of willow skeins.

A similar sieve is also used for grading potatoes, being especially made with the openings in the mesh of uniform size. The measurements vary from $\frac{2}{3}$ inch to $1\frac{7}{8}$, or sometimes to 2 inches.

Fruit-picking Baskets, which can be strapped to the back of the picker, are used for apples and pears in the Evesham district and elsewhere.

Many kinds of agricultural baskets are made either of brown or white rods. Some buyers prefer to pay for the extra cost of white rods as these resist the damp better than do the unpeeled sort, and therefore last longer. A half sieve, costing 3s. 6d. or 4s. of white rods would cost only 3s. if made of brown. Carlisle Swills of willow and cane cost 3s. 9d. or 4s. for the white variety, but could be bought in the autumn, made from the newly cut ' green ' rods, for 3s.

§ 2. *Baskets for Transport Purposes*

Of baskets used for transport purposes the most important are those in which fruit and market-garden produce are packed for conveyance to the markets. Many thousands of these are used every year, but a large proportion of them are imported from Holland, Belgium, and elsewhere.

Pots are the baskets most in use in the west of England for packing fruit. They are oblong open baskets, generally of brown rods, and wider at the top than at the bottom. This shape is a more convenient one when empty baskets have to be stored or transported, as they fit into one another and thus save space. But when the baskets are full of fruit there is danger of damage to the contents if one pot is stood upon another. This is obviated by piling the filled baskets crosswise. The pot holds up to 72 lb. of fruit, according to the variety. The same kind of basket is made in Yorkshire, of brown rods with a stripe of white ones, and is there called a Hamper.

Sieves, which are round baskets, brown or white, holding one bushel, are used for plums and other fruit in the East Midlands and the south-eastern counties. *Half Sieves* hold half a bushel.

Strikes are used for tomatoes, of which they hold 12 lb. They are generally white.

Flats, for fruit, cucumbers, or watercress, are low, square baskets, generally brown.

Rim Pecks are white baskets, made specially for strawberries and holding 12 lb. They are round and are made with a neck on which, when one basket is piled upon another, the upper basket rests, so that the fruit in the lower basket is not damaged.

Potato Hampers are square baskets, with lids, used for sending potatoes and other vegetables to market. Round baskets are also used sometimes for vegetables.

Baskets used for transporting other farm or garden produce are : *Chicken-crates* or *Poultry Show-baskets*, which have ' fitched ' or openwork sides and are used for sending live birds to market or to shows.

Rabbit Hampers are big square baskets, high enough for dead rabbits to be suspended in them at full length. There are two holes near the top of the basket at each end, through which are thrust the sticks on which the rabbits are slung. A great many of these baskets are made near Thetford to supply a local dealer in rabbits. They also form part of the output of many general basket-makers.

Various other types of hamper are made for packing different kinds of produce, including those used for game and the ' Christmas hamper ' of the size necessary to hold a duck or turkey.

Pigeon Baskets are the speciality of a firm in the southwest of England, who employ twenty men chiefly on this work, of which they seem to have a monopoly.

Fell Crates are big round or square baskets used for packing skins for transport to tanneries.

Wholesale chemists and distilleries make use of a big round basket with a lid, of rough brown work, for packing bottles.

§ 3.   *Work for Factories and Industrial Centres.*

Skep, a word applied in different districts to various kinds of basket, indicates in Yorkshire the very strong and heavy basket used in the textile mills for moving woollen goods, in different stages of manufacture, from one part of the factory to another.   The skep is a square open basket of white rods, 3 ft. to 3 ft. 6 in. in height, and often iron-shod and mounted on wheels or runners.   Many skeps are made by the Leeds Blind School, and others by firms in the industrial towns having several employees.   As the baskets are ordered in considerable quantities, the small scale rural maker seldom seeks these orders.

Baskets of a similar type, known as hampers, are made in rural workshops for the Stroud woollen mills, the Northamptonshire boot factories, and the hosiery factories of Derby and Leicestershire.

Very strong white hampers, with lids, are made for the London Meat Market by rural firms as far distant as the northern boundary of Bedfordshire.

Wicker Covers for jars are made for wine and spirit merchants, brewers, &c., and basket-makers are sometimes employed at the potteries where pickle, jam, and spirit jars are produced, to cover these with wicker work.   During the war similar wicker coverings were made for 18-gallon vitriol jars, but iron carboys stuffed with straw are now more often used for this purpose.

§ 4.   *Baskets for Domestic and other General Uses.*

Certain types of this work are usually made for the wholesale trade, and are retailed by many different shops.   Other kinds are produced by the basket-maker to the private

customer's order. Varieties generally sold by the maker to
the wholesale dealer are :

Buff Shopping Baskets, either barrel shaped or oval. Girls
are often employed on this work, and a few small rural
firms produce these baskets successfully, but great quantities of them are imported. In a market town a local
basket-maker often produces a special type of large, strong,
shopping basket for sale to the wives of the farmers who
come to him for their potato baskets and feeding skeps.

Bicycle Baskets are also made by girls, and are supplied
by the maker to the cycle agents, who retail them.

Furniture, both of wicker and cane is made in the Trent
Valley and at Bridgwater, and by other single firms in
various districts. There are two main types of furniture,
one represented by the ' stick chair ', the making of which
partakes of the nature of carpentry as much as of basketry,
the framework, of stout, whole cane, or of two- or three-
year-old willow ends, being fastened together with nails, and
afterwards covered with cane, rush, or willow. The fitched
chair is ' set up ' like basket work, without the use of nails.
In the making of stick chairs, men are employed on the construction work and girls on the filling in. The making of
fitched chairs is more skilled, the shape being modelled as
the work proceeds.

Fishing Baskets were made until lately by a rural worker
in the neighbourhood of Studley, and supplied by him
wholesale to the fish-hook factories in that town.

Baskets which the small maker in a village or market
town makes for sale direct to the users are, in addition to
the agricultural kinds already mentioned :

Laundry Baskets, known as *Flaskets* in the south-eastern
counties, and as *Cradles* in Notts.

Tradesmen's Delivery Baskets of strong white work.

Hampers of various kinds, including the big ones used by
laundries.

The work of the small-scale country maker includes a good
deal of repairing, such as re-bottoming laundry baskets and
other kinds which have hard wear, repairing wicker furniture
and re-seating chairs with rush or cane. Particularly in
towns where there are many dealers in antique furniture,
there are many rush seats to be supplied to chairs.

Wattle Summer-houses and Wicker Garden-chairs constitute
a considerable part of the summer output of a few makers, but
seem to be a line which has not been taken up by many.
The work is of a rough type, brown rods being used. The

summer-houses are made and dispatched to the customer in sections. Some of this work is done for a firm which, operating all over England, advertises the goods, sends exact measurements and specifications to a rural maker who forwards the work on completion direct to the customer. Thus the village basket-maker is put in touch with buyers whose custom he would otherwise have little chance of obtaining, and any unnecessary transport and storing of the bulky goods is avoided.

§ 5. *Specialities of certain districts.*

The seaport towns have perhaps the greatest number of types of baskets peculiar to them.

The *Fish-basket*, used for carrying the catch from the boats to the quay, is a large strong basket, and may be of willow or of cane, round or square. They may be made in or near the seaport, as at St. Ives or Berwick, or even as far inland as Sutton-on-Trent, whence they are sent to Grimsby.

A special variety of the fish-basket is the *Prickle*, which is used on the Sussex coast. For the ' sticks ' of these baskets, hazel wands or other rods are cut from the hedges.

Yarmouth and Lowestoft have their peculiar types in the *Cran* and the *Swill*, the former used for measuring and the latter for lading fish.

The *Cran* is a measure by which fish is sold, but this basket does not actually exist, as it would be too cumbrous for use. The *Quarter-cran* is a tall, round basket, measuring 14½ in. across the bottom, 14½ in. deep, 17½ in, across the mouth, and 21½ in. diagonally, with a 1½ in. rise in the bottom. It is white, woven of cane and willow, with brown willow stakes, and has fitched sides. Two pieces of white wood are fixed to the ends to take the Government stamp. The quarter-cran holds over two bushels ; it was originally a Scotch measure, but it is now officially recognized in East Anglia.

The *Swill* is a peculiar type of basket, being built from the rim downwards, instead of, as is more usual, from the bottom upwards. Hazel wands as well as willows are used in its construction. It is an oval basket about three feet high, with a hole beneath the rim at each end by which the swill may be gripped for carrying. The very stout rods which form the framework of the basket are used both in rings round the circumference of the swill, and as stakes, coming from the bottom and curved up round the ends.

The word *swill* in the North of England is applied to a different type of basket, made entirely of underwood, as already described.[1] In Carlisle, however, *swill* designated a rough basket of willow or cane which was chiefly sold to Scotland for feeding purposes.

Other seaport varieties are :

Cockle-flats and *Shrimp-beds*, made near Ipswich.

Salmon Baskets, made for Bristol fish merchants.

Lobster-pots, which in Cornwall and Sussex are made by the fishermen themselves.

Eel-grigs are made in the Severn valley, and at Boston, Holbeach, and the Wisbech district of Lincs., near the rivers Witham, Welland, and Nene. The eel-grigs are laid in the rivers in the summer when the eels are ' running '. They are long vessels with splayed out, fitched brim, and body of close wicker work, curved into a narrow ' waist ' in the middle. Downward pointing spikes, of strong pieces of willow rod, fixed round this narrow passage, prevent the escape of the eel when it has penetrated to the lower part of the trap. Below the ' waist ' the basket bulges out again, to contain the eels, and is narrowed again at the bottom to a small opening which can be stopped with a wooden plug.

Eel-grigs are troublesome to make, so only a few men will bother to do them ; the demand is not great ; one maker may sell a dozen or two in a season.

Agricultural baskets peculiar to certain districts are :

Oval Bushel Baskets for fruit, instead of the more usual round ones, are made by a firm in Kent.

Broccoli Crates are characteristic of Cornwall, and are large, roughly made, brown baskets, which last two seasons.

Rips are bushel baskets used by Sussex market-gardeners.

Cheese Baskets are made at Bridgwater for the local cheese industry.

Potato Pads are one-hundredweight baskets used in the Potton district of Bedfordshire for early potatoes.

Carrot Skeps or *Scuttles* are similar to potato pickers, but have two small handles, one at either side, instead of one handle over the top, which would be in the way of the carrots. They are made and used in the carrot-growing area around Chatteris.

The *Peck Cob* is a basket used on Suffolk farms. It is white, round in shape, but slightly bellied, and provided with a handle.

---

[1] *The Rural Industries of England and Wales*, vol. i, chap. vii.

F

Stable Skeps, round, splayed-out baskets, of white rods, very strongly made, seem to be a speciality of Newmarket.

A domestic basket, characteristic of a special locality, is the *Southport Boat*, a market basket used by countrywomen in Lancashire, which is of buff rods, ' spelked ', or built from the rim downwards, instead of from the bottom upwards.

A list [1] of journeymen's piece rates for Plymouth and Penzance, published in 1915, which is a reprint of a similar publication of 1887, with the rates revised, gives an interesting list of the different kinds made nearly forty years ago in that district.   Most of the rates had risen by $\frac{1}{2}d.$ per article on the former rates.   About one hundred and twenty kinds of baskets are enumerated as having been made in 1887, including those for fruit, fish (many kinds), coal, lime, and cement; hen-coops, bird-cages, panniers, 'prickles, maunds, baskets and flaskets, reticules, hampers '.   The number of kinds made in 1915 had dwindled to fifty.

As regards the distribution of the various kinds of baskets, the specialities mentioned in § 5 above are made only in certain districts for local use.   The ordinary agricultural baskets are made in nearly every rural district in England, but dairy farming and the production of hay give rise to fewer demands for baskets than the cultivation of potatoes or of fruit.   In a district such as South Cornwall, where the chief output consists of potato pickers, broccoli crates, and fish baskets, it is found that the men engaged constantly on this heavy work have hands unsuited to the manipulation of finer rods in more delicate work, and little or no attempt is made to find any sale for baskets of the latter type.   In the Trent Valley there are found specialists in every type of basket, from the heaviest whole cane work to the finest fancy baskets of ' skeined ' work, but the same firms seldom produce both types.   The single-handed village or market town basket-maker really needs to be the most versatile workman of all, for he may be called upon to make anything, from the heaviest type of farmer's basket to a well-finished shopping basket.   In practice, however, most country folk are more likely to buy a cheap basket of foreign make from a fancy shop in the town than to go to the local maker for

---

[1] ' Revised and enlarged list of the sizes of Basket Work with the Journeymen's Prices affixed as they are made in Plymouth and Devonport and agreed upon at a General Meeting of the Journeymen and approved of by the Master Basket Makers.   Held May 22 1915.'   Fourth Edition. Hopkins, Plymouth.

a light basket, but the imported article often finds its way before long to the village workshop for repairs.

VIII. *Substitutes for Baskets.*

There are certain substitutes which tend to replace baskets for some of their purposes, the most important being the 'non-returnable empties' for the fruit and vegetables sent to Covent Garden and other markets.

Some 90 per cent. of the baskets used in England for orchard and market-garden produce are the property of the salesmen. The Evesham and Hereford districts are exceptional, for there a considerable number of the growers find their own empties, yet even in this case the market authorities are able to dictate to a certain extent.

The salesman, in the first instance, orders baskets from the maker or importer, who paints the owner's name or mark upon them and sends them to the grower. On each basket which the grower returns full to the market he is charged for hire. In 1923 the charge in the Evesham district was 2d. per pot. The price of a pot was 2s. 7d., and a representative firm of Covent Garden salesmen estimates that the life of a basket is three years, making five journeys a year. During the war and until recently, when transport 'facilities' were hardly worthy of that name, and when, owing to pressure of traffic, the baskets received very rough treatment, they only made about three journeys a year, and lasted no more than three years or perhaps not so long. A 'journey' means the transport of the basket from the grower to the market, from the market to the retailer (with possibly an extra stage from central market to local market, and thence to retailer), from retailer back to salesman as an 'empty', and thence again to the grower to be re-filled. At the rate of fifteen journeys at 2d. a time the basket will ultimately be paid for by the grower on the instalment system.

Thus a large part of the salesman's capital is sunk in baskets, but they represent a definite link between himself and the grower, on one hand, and between himself and the retailer, on the other hand, and it is advantageous to him to have these comparatively permanent receptacles distributed amongst them, for the basket can only be returned to the man whose name is marked on them. 'Non-returnable empties', on the other hand, are not marked with the salesman's name because this would not be worth the expense, and, in some cases, as with nets, it would be very difficult to do. The returnable empty assists in the establishment of salesmen's trade connexions, especially with growers, in a way in which the other cannot.

Most fruit travels better in baskets, excepting hard fruit, such as apples, for which barrels are largely used. For cherries and plums baskets are generally admitted to be superior. The salesman may incur some expense for the repair of baskets and for the storage of them in winter. There is also the trouble of booking them as they are issued and returned. There is some danger of loss by pilfering, or by careless treatment of the basket by the grower or retailer. During the winter, considerable numbers of baskets can be seen piled up in orchards without shelter, and distressing tales are told of how they are used by the retailers as dust bins and for other purposes for which they were not intended. But a salesman stated that the amount of loss through theft or damage is now very small, inspectors being employed to travel about the country and ensure that the baskets receive proper treatment. It has already been seen that nearly the whole original cost of the basket is eventually repaid by the grower, and on the whole the salesman finds that baskets are more advantageous for him and cheaper in the long run than non-returnable empties.

It is the man who buys fruit or vegetables for retail in his shop who prefers the non-returnable package. The Evesham custom is that when he buys produce in pots he is charged for the pot a sum that is refunded on its return to the market. The amount charged may vary from a sum slightly below the value of the pot, if the buyer is well known, to more than its actual value if he is a new buyer. The general principle is the same in other districts. Thus, the buyer has the trouble and expense of returning the basket in good condition to the salesman, and therefore it is sometimes found that retailers will more readily buy, and will pay a higher price for, produce in non-returnable packages.

In the Evesham district, when nets or bags are used, the grower is charged for the nets at the rate of 7d. or 8d. a piece when he takes them from the market, this being a great deal more than the actual value. When he returns the nets full, the amount paid is refunded to him with the deduction of 1d. each for hire. The high charge is made to ensure the return of the nets, as the market authorities have no other hold upon them. For the use of pots, which are marked with the owner's name, the grower is only charged when he returns them filled. Nets of coco-nut fibre are used for cabbages, and string bags for brussels sprouts. The retailer who buys produce put up in nets has to buy the net outright, and therefore dislikes this method of packing, but as the use of the net prevents ' topping ' (i. e. the packing of the better produce on top and the inferior stuff below), some salesmen prefer nets. When there is a plentiful supply of cabbages and the salesmen thus obtain control of the market, they will issue an order that no baskets are to be used. Nets are also used in South Cornwall.

Another type of non-returnable empty is the wooden box or case. This, like the net, is much cheaper than the basket, but in the long run it costs the salesman more. The retailer prefers this kind of package, as it can be broken up and some use made of the boards. The pre-war price of a wooden box was $3\frac{1}{2}d$. for the bushel size, and $2\frac{1}{2}d$. for a half-bushel box. It was said that the retailers would pay $6d$. more on each bushel of fruit in a wooden non-returnable case. Round vessels of bent-wood are used by some salesmen for tomatoes, and cost $2\frac{3}{4}d$., whereas the strike which they replace costs $1s.$ $6d.$ The strike, however, outlasts about fifteen of the non-returnable packages, so the latter are relatively dear. Another package used for tomatoes is a square box of wooden slats with spaces between, which was introduced recently by a Covent Garden firm and at once gained popularity. During the war, and for two or three years after, the high cost of wood caused a diminution in the use of wooden vessels, but in 1923 they were already coming into favour again. Disused margarine boxes and other empties may be bought cheaply, and are used by some salesmen. Collapsible wooden crates were formerly used in South Cornwall, in addition to the wicker crates, and may again replace the latter partly or entirely. Wicker crates, however, seem to preserve the produce in better condition than any substitute can do.

The use of road transport helps to simplify the problem of returning empties, for they can travel back on top of another load at no extra expense. Non-returnable packages, particularly nets, are lighter than baskets, so the freightage on them is less. All salesmen are interested in the question of the non-returnable empty and the possibility of devising some substitute for the basket, which would be considerably cheaper and yet carry the fruit as efficiently.

For packing strawberries and other small fruit the chip basket is a favourite form of package ; if the fruit travels by sea, as from the Channel Isles, and has to be moved by crane, something stronger than the chip basket is needed. But for ordinary use, some salesmen consider that there is nothing to beat the open chip basket, because, being frail, it receives more careful handling than a wicker basket.

Chip baskets were, before the war, imported in large numbers from Sweden, but during the war years the factories which had been started in England shortly before increased their production to such an extent that they now supply a very large proportion of the chip baskets which are in use. There are several of these factories in England, some at Wisbech, one in Hampshire, others in the Tamar Valley and at Swanwick and Cheddar—all centres of the strawberry growing areas. There are others on the outskirts of London, in Glasgow, and elsewhere. These industries are on a large scale, elaborate machinery is used, and the only hand work is highly specialized, and takes the form of very simple processes. It is light work, carried out chiefly by girls, and provides the utmost contrast to the craft of wicker basket-making.[1] The material used is thin shavings of wood, cut from Russian aspen and also from certain kinds of English timber, such as poplar, willow, and Scotch fir. A factory employing one hundred girls can produce five hundred gross of chip baskets weekly.

Other packages which are sometimes used for fruit and vegetables in preference to the English wicker basket are, apart from the new Dutch baskets, which are imported in great numbers,[2] foreign baskets which come from Belgium, Holland, and elsewhere, filled with lettuces, butter, and other produce ; these are sold very cheaply in the English market as empties. Such baskets are probably only used by the smaller dealers, since the supply of any particular size would be uncertain, but the English makers maintain that this system of sending produce to England in baskets which can be sold here at a very low price is on the increase, and is detrimental to their industry. These foreign empties are sometimes bought by farmers for use as potato pickers, or even by private people for use as shopping baskets. They are often of poor quality, and may have to go at once to an English maker for repairs, but the buyer is elated by the feeling that he has a bargain, even if, by the time the basket has been re-bottomed and fitted with a new handle, he has spent as much on it as a more substantial English one would have cost him.

[1] See Part II of this volume, Chapter III, *Some Rural Factories.*
[2] See Section IX, p. 71, *Foreign Competition.*

Farmers make some use of zinc receptacles for feeding beasts, in place of wood scuttles or other baskets. Zinc feeders cost less in the beginning, but they will not last so long as scuttles, being easily damaged and not repairable. The labourers dislike them because they are unpleasant to handle in cold weather.

Baskets were at one time used for packing fish, but now that fish is usually packed in ice, barrels and boxes are used, and generally the baskets are only needed for carrying the fish from the boats to the quay.

IX. *Foreign Competition.*

Foreign competition is one of the most important factors in the future development of the basket-making industry in England. It is no new difficulty, but its effect is probably more strongly felt now than at any time before. It affected the industry considerably before 1870, and old basket-makers remember that there was a great boom of the trade in England during that year, owing to the fact that the Franco-Prussian war interfered with the export of baskets to England from France and Germany. A certain firm in Yorkshire had about forty journeymen at that time, but by 1914 the number had fallen to twenty, and at present there is only one man regularly employed, and another engaged occasionally at busy seasons. There has been a steady increase in the number of imported baskets up to the beginning of the European War, and since the imports have been resumed they have again increased. In 1910 and 1911 the imports from Belgium were the largest, and the amount remained steady in 1912 and 1913, when the imports from Japan had increased to a figure above that for Belgium. The imports from the Netherlands, next in value to those from Belgium, decrease slightly from 1910 to 1913, but rise again rapidly in 1914, when imports from Belgium began to fall off owing to the outbreak of war. The steady increase in the quantity of baskets sent from Japan is a remarkable point, but these imports are, for the most part, not wicker-work, but baskets and bags of a sort of rush or grass, and very light fancy baskets of split bamboo. Their influence upon the English basket industry is therefore less than that of the imports from Belgium and Holland.

During the war the Dutch baskets, which had already become a serious menace to the English industry in the particular line of sieves, gained an even firmer footing. The supply of Belgian, French, and German kinds was stopped, and this gave more work to the English makers, but at the same time not only were many makers called to the colours, but many others had to make shell baskets for the munition factories. Fruit and produce salesmen needed more baskets than usual, because transport facilities were so much reduced that it was a long time before baskets once sent out were returned. It was impossible to obtain enough English baskets for packing fruit, so the Dutch were increasingly used. The big firms of importers established their stalls in Covent Garden market and became well known. Nine-tenths of the pots now used in Evesham are said to be Dutch. These foreign baskets were originally very inferior, and for some time after the Dutch makers had succeeded in producing satisfactory round baskets (sieves), they failed to make the square shapes (flats and pots) well. After the war, therefore, the salesmen at first welcomed the return to the market of the English basket, and there was a temporary boom in the English industry. But the Dutch were pro-ducing at prices lower than the English and at the same time improving the quality of their work. In 1920 most salesmen spoke of the inferiority of the Dutch baskets, and thought that there was a good future for the English makers ; by 1923 the Dutch baskets were considered as in no way inferior to the English, and perhaps even better. In fact, some of the English work had deteriorated, owing to the efforts made to speed up the work in order to compete, whilst the falling off in the quality of the English rods aggravated this.

It is of the utmost importance to the Covent Garden sales-men to get the best baskets, for they are subject to very rough usage during transport, and therefore need to be of the strongest kind. The allegation of some basket-makers that the salesman will always buy the cheapest basket, no matter how poor the quality, because in any case it does not outlast one season, does not seem to be justified. While the quality of English work remained good, and there seemed some prospect that the foreigner might be beaten, there were certain salesmen who subsidized English firms and took all their output in spite of its much higher price.

Certain Dutch firms have basket warehouses in the chief fruit-growing centres, such as the Maidstone district, in which they stock large quantities of baskets. When orders are received from a salesman his name and mark is painted on the baskets and they are sent out to the grower, as they would be from an English maker. Further, the Dutch warehouse will, for a charge, store the baskets during the winter months. The Dutch firm thus fulfils all the functions of the English maker, and the additional one, very useful to the salesman, of providing a winter storehouse. Salesmen who buy Dutch baskets from firms which only have agents in London, have their own storehouses in the neighbourhood of the orchards, at Maidstone, Wisbech, and elsewhere, in which they keep the baskets when not in use.

Nearly every kind of basket for which there is any considerable demand in wholesale quantities is now imported, and there is hardly a maker who has not, within the last thirty years, had to yield up some particular wholesale order to the foreigner. German baskets are chiefly of the small fancy kinds, and the workmanship, as a rule, is poor. Some of the Belgian work also is rough, but some is good. The Belgian refugees are said not only to have learnt the art of buffing in England, but also to have taken English patterns of baskets with them when they returned home, and the quality of their work seems to be improving, but the agricultural baskets which they send are still very ' slender '—not fit for hard wear. French baskets are chiefly of the fancy or domestic kinds. Much of the French work is expensive, but it is of excellent workmanship and unequalled in its own class. There is generally a ready sale for it in the better class town shops, and much of it is of a type not produced in England. Many of their fancy baskets of delicate workmanship, ' skeined '—i. e. of fine skeins, each woven in separately, not slewed—are probably made by women, and, owing to the fineness of the skeins, the work must take considerable time.

The kinds of baskets chiefly imported are as follows :

Nearly all those used for the transport of fruit and vegetables, but fewer flats than other kinds.

Potato pickers which come from Belgium are generally of rougher workmanship than the English kind, and in Yorkshire it was said that they were getting less popular. Nevertheless, five thousand were sold in the small town of Howden in the autumn of 1922. Frequently they were auctioned. There is a great variety of opinion about this particular type of basket, some people saying that the farmer would never buy anything but English pickers if he could get enough of these when they are needed. But it is convenient for him to wait until the women are actually upon the land, when he can estimate his requirements exactly, and then it is often found that insufficient English baskets are available. Some firms state that the Belgian picker has entirely ousted the English basket, and they have given up making this kind ; but retailers sometimes say that the demand for Belgian and for English pickers is about equal. Some makers of agricultural baskets put in all their spare time throughout the year on pickers, being sure of a sale for them, and one declared that he could get as many orders from Norfolk for pickers as he liked to take, although the price paid is low. The conclusion seems to be that English makers could compete fairly successfully with the Belgians in this line if they had more enterprise and more capital, so that they could take the risk of making for stock, and thus provide a sufficient supply at the moment when they are needed, without giving the farmer the trouble of ordering in advance.

Potato skips are also imported, and hampers for potatoes and for other purposes. These kinds, and laundry baskets, are particularly suitable for import, because, being wider at the top, they pack easily into one another, and so save space. Laundry baskets are imported in very large quantities, some of those from Germany being of the wretchedest material, dark in colour, with rods of various sizes used together, some of them being little better than straw.

Other kinds of agricultural baskets do not come from abroad, as they are not usually required in wholesale quantities and are also less standardized than other kinds, special patterns being preferred in different districts.

The cheaper varieties of wicker furniture are imported, similar to the type made in Bridgwater. The Belgians have the additional advantage that the rush plait, used in this work and in fancy baskets, is now produced much more cheaply in Belgium, and is also imported for the use of English basket-makers. The foreign furniture is lighter in weight than the English, so that less material is used in the making of it, and the transport is cheaper.

The reasons for the relative cheapness of foreign baskets, as far as they can be ascertained, may be summarized as follows :

1. Cheapness of material. In Holland, particularly, there are great tracts of land suitable to the production of osiers, though not of those of the best quality. These are cultivated by big firms on a large scale, which sell the rods to the workers and buy the finished baskets from them.

2. Cheapness of labour. In 1922, a basket-maker's earn-

ings in Holland averaged the equivalent of 28s. a week. This is due to several causes.

(a) The employment of family labour, members of a family being in the position of a group of outworkers for a large firm.

(b) The low standard of living among the workers and the long hours worked.

(c) Lack of organization among the workers and no Trade Union rates of wages.

(d) The employment of semi-skilled workers and of women and children on the lighter work, such as the preparing of material. This method is made easy by the system of family work.

(e) The utilization, in France and Holland, of the spare time of workers employed on the land during part of the year.

3. Specialization. This is illustrated by the story of two German workmen who were engaged by an English firm before the war. It was found that they could only make chair backs, but either one of them could make three of these while an English worker was making two.

4. The large scale organization and concentration of the outworkers in certain villages in Holland, which facilitates the collection of work by the firms which buy it from these home workers. This system of large firms which produce the material, sell it to the home workers, buy the finished product from them and re-sell it on a large scale, is probably the most economical in an industry of this kind, in which machinery cannot be used, and in which the whole outfit required is so simple. This system of production eliminates the profits of the small middlemen.

5. Cheap sea transport. Foreign competition in baskets, other than those for fruit and vegetable transport, is felt most severely in the districts round London and near Hull, Wisbech, and other ports to which the baskets come direct by sea.

Cane and wicker furniture of first-class quality and original design, especially of the type used in clubs and cafés, seems to be the only kind that is practically immune from foreign competition. Large firms can more easily adapt themselves to the changing markets and take up new work when necessary, so they are apt to suffer less than the small ones. The makers of sieves, pots, and other kinds of baskets for the transport of produce are the worst hit, and men who have done only this type of heavy work cannot easily turn to other kinds. The small scale maker of general basket work for sale in towns also suffers badly, for the foreign baskets are stocked by so many retailers, such as ironmongers, fancy and toy shops, and furniture dealers. In a certain very small town there were three shops stocking a considerable quantity of imported baskets in opposition to one maker who sold his own wares in his own shop. In larger towns the proportion would be much larger.

Makers of baskets for local farmers suffer least of all, particularly the makers of local specialities, such as scuttles, for which there is always a certain demand.

Town makers who have shops of their own can deal in foreign baskets, and thus make up for the loss of market for their own products. Many find that not only is it more profitable to deal in baskets than to make them, but also that more money can be made on the sale of foreign than of English makes. A retailer who had stocks of both English and Belgian potato pickers, stated that he made $\frac{1}{2}d$. more profit on the sale of each Belgian picker at 2s. than on the English variety at 3s. 4d.   In Yorkshire it was said that men who had started business by peddling foreign baskets on foot had, within a year or so, made enough profit to enable them to travel round in a motor van. Many of the largest firms of basket manufacturers also deal in foreign baskets, and the smaller firms, who buy from them for retail purposes, are often ignorant as to whether certain baskets are English or foreign. A Hull firm, which formerly had a basket industry in that town, is now said to have a factory in Holland.

Some dealers in foreign baskets keep a skilled workman employed in repairing and 'finishing' these—cutting off rough ends of material, strengthening handles, and so forth. A certain small maker of general basket-work always buys foreign shopping baskets, and after improving the setting-in of the handles, sells them in his shop with his own produce, and considers that they are equal to similar baskets of his own make, which would cost him more.

Foreign competition in rods does not severely affect the English basketry and osier industries in their rural aspect. Of the imported rods, the French seem to be the best, but, like the French baskets, they are of a type which is seldom produced in England. They are used by town makers to some extent for fine work, and are liked by them for their qualities of whiteness and smoothness. The Dutch and Belgian rods which are sent to England are of a cheaper,

BASKET MAKING

CHAIR CANING

rougher kind, but owing to the fact that they are better
sorted than some of the English rods of similar quality,
they may prove serious rivals to these latter. At the time
when the investigations were made, however, few rural
makers seemed to be using them. The Trent Valley growers,
who not only produce some of the finest osiers in the world,
but who also understand the value of careful preparation
and sorting, probably have little to fear from foreign competition, but the Somerset growers, and those in other
districts, whose standards are not so high, may find it
necessary to take more trouble in details of this kind in
order to retain their market.

X. *Marketing of Baskets.*

Considered in relation to the markets which they supply,
basket-making firms may be classified as those who deal
only with the wholesale trade and those who supply baskets
retail to local buyers. There are also some who supply both
markets.

Firms of the first class are found chiefly in the districts
where basket-making is carried out on the largest scale and
who specialize in certain types of work, such as the Trent
Valley and the Bridgwater district. Bridgwater chairs are
sold to South Wales ironmongers and hardware manufacturers, and also to furniture dealers elsewhere. In the
Trent Valley there are middlemen who buy cane in large
quantities and store it for retail to the small makers, from
whom these firms also buy the baskets made, storing these
and re-selling them when the market is most favourable.
These middlemen are thus particularly useful to the small
maker of some special variety of basket, for which the
demand might be a somewhat fluctuating one, for they
ensure to him the regular sale for his output which is essential
for the firm with small capital. Other makers sell to retailing
or manufacturing firms in the district or elsewhere.

The small rural firms which manufacture farmers' baskets,
usually retail direct to local customers, but if any speciality
is made for which there is also a demand in other districts,
such as the wood-scuttle, this particular variety may also
be made to the order of large wholesale dealers. The village
basket-maker may have a little shop in which to display his
wares, or, since his customers are regular ones who know
him well, he may rely on their coming to his workshop when
they need his baskets. He may supply a few ironmongers'

shops in neighbouring towns with some kinds, particularly potato pickers. In some counties, particularly in Lincolnshire, a basket-maker frequently has a stall at one or more of the local markets. In the south-western counties, where single-handed basket-makers in towns were doing very badly and the output of some of them exceeded the local demand, they had taken to hawking their wares in the seaside towns during the summer.

The makers of fruit and transport baskets may actually sell these to salesmen in very distant towns to which the produce of the district is sent, but the basket goes direct from the maker to the grower who is about to fill it, and therefore the effect is that the basket-maker is supplying local customers.[1] In South Cornwall the baskets are largely owned by the growers themselves, so the actual purchasers are people in the district, but the Worcestershire pot hamper-maker probably deals with a salesman in Manchester or Birmingham, and the Fen Country sieve-maker with a Covent Garden or Sheffield salesman.

Basket-making was certainly never an industry in which small scale makers were likely to reap large profits. Osier-growing is more speculative and gives more chance of large returns. A scuttle-maker in Yorkshire mentioned a brother in the same industry who died worth £5,000 ; this man had set up in business independently as a young man with hardly any capital, but his father was a farmer, and he thus obtained land for a willow garth on favourable terms. He cultivated the rods chiefly for his own use, but possibly sold some of them in years when they would fetch a good price. He was thus working under the most favourable conditions possible, with facilities for the cheap production of material near at hand, opportunity for selling his surplus material—if he had any—profitably, and the fact that he was a skilled maker of a particular variety of basket for which there was a steady demand, exceeding the supply. The case, however, is certainly an unusual one, and very few rural makers are able to accumulate wealth to anything like this extent.

Small makers who have no shops of their own often complain that the local retailer, to whom they sell some of their output, makes an unfair profit upon it. Thus an East Anglian maker stated that he sold some agricultural baskets to a retailer at 11d. each, and later saw the same baskets exposed for sale in the shop in Norwich at 1s. 9d. each, representing a profit of 91 per cent. An East Midland master

1 See Section VIII, p. 67, *Substitutes for Baskets.*

basket-maker, whose daughter was learning to make shopping baskets, sold a number which were slightly defective in shape to a retailer for 1s. 3d. each, and later heard that they were nearly all disposed of for 3s. 9d. each, a profit of 200 per cent., which seems excessive, even taking into account the fact that only a small profit might be made on a few of the most defective ones. Retailers, however, state that they can almost always make more profit on foreign than on English baskets, and therefore prefer to stock the former. The cases mentioned may be exceptional, but it is certainly true that both wholesale and retail prices of baskets seem to vary considerably from time to time, and even over a fairly small area, the unorganized rural makers selling at high or low prices, according to their immediate financial conditions.

XI. *General Conclusions and Prospects.*

The two industries of osier-growing and basket-making are, by their very nature, closely connected and inter-dependent. The fact that there is no considerable export from England of either rods or baskets, renders the inter-dependence more complete, although the *import* of rods does give the basket-maker an alternative source of supply. The osier-grower, however, is by no means entirely dependent upon the rural side of the basketry industry—the only part of it which is dealt with in this survey. There is a con-siderable body of urban basket-makers, whose problems and outlook probably differ widely from those of their brother craftsmen in the country, and who would provide a market for the English rods of better quality, even if the rural industry died out.

This investigation of rural industries was begun when the period of prosperity which followed the war was beginning to decline into the slump which lasted, with increasing severity, until the survey was completed in 1923. It is probably the worst which the basket industry has ever known. It was therefore difficult at the conclusion of the survey to estimate the prospects of revival. In 1920 fruit salesmen were generally optimistic as to the future of the English pot and sieve industry. In 1923 most of them summed it up briefly as ' dead '. In 1920 it was thought by many authorities to be desirable to plant another hundred acres or so of osiers in England. By 1923 many of the beds belonging to the smaller growers were falling year by year into a state of worse dereliction, because there was so little demand for the rods at the price necessary to repay the cost of cultivation, that the growers could not afford to sink more money in the beds. Thus the rods became poorer in quality, and the growers became increasingly unable to spend anything on the improvement of the crop.

The beds of the bigger growers, however, were still in good condition, and undoubtedly there was a fairly steady demand for rods of the higher grades. The more important growers, who depend least on the village basket-maker for their market, seem to have a future before them. The small growers, particularly those beyond the noted willow-growing areas, suffered most from the difficult conditions of the years 1921–3. It has been shown that the cost of maintaining osier-beds in good condition, apart from the initial cost of planting according to the best methods, is considerable. The cost of labour is the chief factor, and there is therefore little possibility of reduction. Obviously, the small grower without capital cannot afford the outlay necessary for the production of the best rods, and cannot, therefore, hope to supply any but the local village makers who need rods of moderate price for their rougher work. These makers have to meet the competition of cheap foreign baskets and of certain cheap substitutes for baskets, such as the non-returnable empties and the zinc vessels used for cattle feeding, and therefore it is important for them to be able to obtain rods of fair quality at the lowest possible price. Somerset growers have, during recent years, considerably developed their trade beyond their own locality, and seem to be becoming the main source of supply to the rural basket-maker, in so far as his needs are not met by local growers. The Somerset rods would meet his demands even more adequately if more trouble were taken to sort them carefully and to supply rods exactly in accordance with orders.

On the whole, there seems to be little possibility of development for that particular branch of the osier-growing industry represented by the small isolated grower who is not also a basket-maker. Obviously he cannot hope to produce good enough rods to compete against the Trent Valley firms. On the other hand, there are often other rods grown in his neighbourhood, on farms and large estates, where they are planted mainly to provide cover for game and to utilize otherwise worthless land. These growers hardly look for profit from their osiers, and can therefore sell at lower prices than the grower who has to make a living from his holt. The village basket-maker, being anxious to lower his costs of production as far as possible, will buy the farmer's rods because, although of poor quality, they are just good enough to serve his purpose. Moreover, if he is in a position to cut and prepare the rods himself, he can further economize by buying a standing crop from the farmer. The professional grower is often reluctant to sell his rods in this way, owing to the possibility of damage being done to the stocks by careless cutting. For rods of a slightly superior quality, which the farmer cannot supply, the village maker sends to Somerset rather than to a local grower, because the wholesale merchant can, from his large stock, send all the kinds needed, whereas it might be necessary to approach two or three small growers in order to obtain, for example, some soft rods for scuttle-making, some buffed material for shopping baskets, and some strong white rods for feeding-skeps.

The many small country makers who grow their own rods find this method of obtaining material the most economical of all, so long as they can supply themselves with what they need. This accounts for the fact that in some districts there is undoubtedly an unsatisfied demand on the part of the basket-makers for small plots of land, within easy distance of their workshops, for osier-growing, whilst at the same time there are many moderate-sized beds which are running to waste. As regards the joint makers and growers, their future prospects as basket-makers is the point of chief importance. The decline of the rural side of the basketry industry is more widespread than in the case of osier-growing, not being limited to small isolated makers. The following examples, taken from the East Midland district, are typical cases from areas which have felt the foreign competition most severely :

Ely. In one firm which employed as many as fifty men before the war, there were seven men working during the few busiest weeks of 1922, and only two later in the year. Early in 1923 the workshop was closed down, with the faint chance that it might be re-opened later in the season.

St. Neots (Hunts.). There used to be thirty men employed in the industry here. Early in 1923 there were three.

Woodstone (Peterborough). One firm, which employed sixty men before the war, had eight or nine on half time in 1923.

Biggleswade (Beds.). There were formerly from thirty to

forty men making baskets in this town, and in the spring of 1923 there were seven.

Leighton Buzzard (Beds.). One firm employed sixty men before the war and up to the end of June 1921 ; thirty were then dismissed, and most of the rest had been turned off by ones and twos until, in May 1923, only three were at work on a small order, with the prospect of dismissal on its completion.

Feltham. One maker used to execute orders for a number of big firms of fruit salesmen and market-gardeners. They would each order about three thousand baskets every year, and there were also many smaller orders. In 1922 his sale averaged, at the outside, fifty baskets a week over the whole year, one thousand of these being for one firm which used to take three thousand annually, and the remaining one thousand five hundred being made up of small orders for from ten to twenty dozen each.

The following figures were given in the West of England to illustrate the decline of the pot-hamper industry there :

	Number of Journeymen.	
	Pre-war.	1921.
Worcester	60	about 20
Evesham and Pershore . . .	100-120	barely 20
One Pershore firm	27	5
One Evesham firm	14	6
Gloucestershire, district near Evesham	207	37

A firm in Stratford-on-Avon which formerly employed fifty men, had, in 1923, declined to the position of one, in which only members of the family were employed, with occasional help from a journeyman. Of the firms established in Kent about 1840, for the manufacture of sieves, hardly one now survives.

Another side of the situation in the basket industry is, however, to be seen in the Bridgwater wicker industry, where development in a new direction has caused its survival. The wicker-furniture making in that district was started when there was a slump in other branches of the basket trade, about twenty years ago, and the industry seems to have a future. In other districts, where no new line has been developed to replace those for which the market has been lost, the whole basket industry is dwindling.

In every district the number of small rural makers seems to be on the decrease ; even before the war there was a tendency for master basket-makers to apprentice their sons to some other trade, if they could afford to do so, although it is also true that the present generation of makers can often boast of a long line of forefathers in the same industry. It often happens that when the old village basket-maker dies no one takes his place, for where there are so many single-handed workers, if the son is not ready to do this there is no one else. In a district where the number of makers thus diminishes, it may happen that the few who remain are enabled to make a better livelihood than they have done for some time previously. At the same time, whilst old businesses die out, new ones are started, although not in sufficiently large numbers to make up the balance. Basket-makers in rural districts often seem to prefer to earn their livelihood in independence, even though it may necessitate long hours of work, to the position of a journeyman. Where large basket industries have been compelled to close down, or at least to reduce the number of their employees, a number of the men who are turned off may set up in business on their own account in the same locality, and although there is little chance for the development of these one-man businesses, the maker may contrive to earn a livelihood for himself, eked out, perhaps, by seasonal labour on the land.

There seem to be three main causes for the decline of the basket industry—the growing use of non-returnable empties, foreign competition, and a certain amount of competition from other substitutes for baskets. As regards non-returnable empties, the whole situation seems to be in the melting pot. It is possible that the undoubted superiority, in many respects and for many purposes, of the baskets over other forms of package may lead to their retention to a greater extent than has seemed likely at some moments when some new type of cheap non-returnable empty has taken the market by storm. The other two difficulties can, it would seem, be combated only by the maintenance of a high standard of work. It might seem, on the face of it, to be ridiculous that the basket-maker who grows his willows and has his workshop beside the orchard whose produce his baskets are made to hold, who has, moreover, an opportunity for utilizing in winter the labour which is employed in those same orchards during the summer, cannot compete with firms abroad whose baskets must travel so far by land and water to the place where they are to be used. Both the Employers' Federation and the Basket-makers' Union seem to believe that protection would be a remedy against foreign competition, and the two bodies have made repeated demands for a tariff of 33 per cent. on foreign baskets. They maintain that the imposition of such a tariff would enable the English makers to compete with the foreigner in certain types of work. For instance, fruit pots of English make were sold in Worcestershire in 1923 at 2s. 7d. each, and the suggested tariff would raise the price of Dutch pots to 3s. In some work, however, the disparity of cost is so extreme that even a tariff would be of little use. For example, Belgian laundry baskets were sold in this country in 1923 at 18s. a dozen ; the addition of 33 per cent. would bring this price up to 24s. 6d. The cost of production of the same type of basket was then 30s. 8½d. a dozen in England, and the addition of the necessary 20 per cent. profit raises this to 36s. 10d. This type of foreign basket is of poor quality, and a policy of co-operation between the osier-grower and the basket-maker, to enable the maker to get exactly the rods he needs, and thus to improve the standard of work, is more likely to have a beneficial effect on the industry than any tariff. Moreover, a large number of the cheaper kinds of foreign baskets are sold by shops which do not stock those of English make, so that the customer does not have the opportunity of comparing the two, between which there is often an obvious difference of finish and durability, in favour of the English basket. A general recognition of the superiority of the best English work over many of the imported baskets and a less short-sighted policy on the part of many buyers of baskets—who often seek the lowest priced article, regardless of its wearing qualities—would do much to help the industry.

For certain types of English basket-work the demand remains fairly steady, and does not seem likely to suffer any serious diminution. Such, for instance, is the case with the skeps and hampers used in factories, baskets for dock work, farmers' scuttles, feeders, sieves, and other kinds, particularly local specialities, and the general repair work and re-seating of chairs. Tradesmen's delivery baskets are also in constant demand, and the small fruit-grower who markets his own produce and does not need sieves or pots in sufficiently large quantities to be able to buy them from the Dutch importers, still relies on the local maker.

Obviously the basket-maker's supply of material is a vital point in the question of his future prospects. If he grows his own he can supply himself cheaply, but not probably, with the best material. Here he could be helped a great deal if the knowledge which is now common property among

the scientific growers could be brought to him. Organization
would help, but organization amongst scattered rural craftsmen is always difficult. It would enable these small isolated
growers to establish a system of exchange, such as is current
amongst the Trent Valley growers, which would help them
to get rid of any rods they did not need, and to obtain
others of the sort suited to their work at the least possible
cost.

Thorough training in many branches of basketry, together
with some knowledge of willow-growing, is even more necessary for the rural maker, who has to satisfy the demands
of so many different customers, than for the worker in some
large urban firm which produces one type of work for the
wholesale market. In the present state of the industry,
when the village basket-maker, even if he can make a living
for himself, can seldom afford an employee or even an
apprentice, the prospects for the training of the next
generation of rural basket-makers are not very bright. A versatile man has more chance of survival, because not only
may he be able if the market for one type of work fails
to turn to another, but there is also more likelihood that
he may obtain some work for a more distant market which
will fill in the slack seasons when there is little demand for
locally used agricultural baskets. In some districts certain
makers may be found working overtime, whilst others are
drawing unemployment pay, as was the case in Worcester
in 1922. Not only versatility but co-operation between
different branches of the industry is needed to remedy this
state of affairs. Another need in the basket industry is for
more capital, which would enable the rural worker to make
on stock the kinds of baskets, such as potato pickers, which
are needed in large quantities at certain seasons of the year.
Yet in the present uncertain state of the industry it is
impossible to find capital for such an enterprise as this.
Only if it could be assured that the baskets could be sold
at a cost at least no greater than that of the foreign varieties,
which are sure to arrive in due season, would the venture
have any chance of success.

The whole situation in both industries is very intricate,
and a vicious circle is to be found in the fact that, whilst
the basket-maker's necessity for keeping down the cost of
production leads him to seek the cheapest material, the use
of that material lowers the value of his work and renders it
less likely to withstand competition, whilst the maker's
inability to pay high prices for rods, renders the grower

unable to afford the best methods of cultivation, so that the osier-beds deteriorate, and the standard of basketry work is further lowered owing to the poor quality of the rods.

There are certain problems affecting the future of both industries which might be solved by research work undertaken by large firms, but which are beyond the scope of the small grower or basket-maker. As regards the best varieties of rods and the suitability of different types of soil, valuable experimental work has for some time been carried out in the Trent Valley. The possible use of by-products is a problem of which the solution might ensure the future prosperity of both industries. The peeled bark is used as manure in Somerset, and also for stack ' staddling ' ; apart from this no use for it has yet been found, except as a thatching for the stacked rods. Possibly the dye which stains the rods when they are boiled in their skins (buffed), might be extracted from the bark peeled from the white rods. A definite attempt has been made to manufacture paper from willow peelings. The experiments were discontinued during the war owing to the cost of labour. Paper had been produced, but of a coarse and thick kind, creamy in colour, and not of sufficient marketable value in relation to the cost of production. This was considerable, owing, amongst other things, to the labour needed to pick out all the ' snags ' or pieces of stick from the peelings. Further experiments with the bark from different varieties of willows might produce satisfactory results, and if good paper could be made in sufficient quantities to keep a factory busy near any district where willows are extensively grown, it might serve as a means of absorbing labour when work on the holts is slack. It is also possible that some substance coarser than paper, some kind of fibre suitable for mat making, might be manufactured from the peel.

The use of machinery in both industries is a possibility to which much thought has been given, but nothing satisfactory has as yet been devised. It was suggested in Somerset that a reaper might be used for cutting, a light tractor for hoeing, and a machine for cutting and binding the rods. Cutting, however, would be very difficult to carry out by machinery on account of the many different directions in which the rods shoot from the stolls. A reaper which only mowed the shoots level would necessitate hand trimming of the stools afterwards. Moreover, it would be difficult to introduce any machinery between the ranks of a withy bed with its big stumps and many branching rods.

As regards basket-weaving, the difficulty is that willow rods taper and are in short lengths. Much time and ingenuity has been spent in trying to devise some kind of machine which would weave even the easiest part of a simple basket, but so far without success.

Apart from the remote chance of some invention which might open up unexpected possibilities, the prospects for the future development of the rural basketry industry depend upon so many factors that they cannot be estimated with any certainty. The point which stands out most clearly, and that to which all paths of research into the position of both this and the osier-growing industry lead, is the necessity for more co-operation both between individual basket-makers and between the makers and the growers. It seems clear that the small village maker cannot stand alone, and his problems cannot be considered alone. It must be remembered that we have reached a point of time far beyond the period when the village community was self-supporting. The village basket-maker has to meet with competition from outside sources, and therefore he needs support from outside his own immediate locality. He is of great value to the agricultural community—some of his products are almost irreplaceable by any substitutes—but he cannot earn a living by the making of two or three local specialities for which there is only a limited and a seasonal demand. If he is to continue to exist it will be necessary for him, on his own part, to get into closer touch with his fellow craftsmen, and for others concerned with the rural basket industry, either as producers of raw material or as buyers of finished products, to give some thought and to be prepared actively to co-operate in its development.

CHAPTER III

RUSH, SEDGE, AND REED INDUSTRIES

Geographical Distribution.

THE three terms, ' rush ', ' reed ', and ' sedge ', are used indiscriminately in a way which is most confusing, for there are five distinct plants to which the names are properly applied, which are employed for distinct purposes. Many people know the reed apart from the other two, but few even of the rush workers themselves can explain the difference between rush and sedge, although in practice they find it comparatively easy to distinguish between them. The old Norfolk men who make sedge horse-collars, maintain that the only difference between rush and sedge is that the latter, which is bigger and coarser, is a rush at a different stage of growth. The difference in the appearance of reeds and rushes, it is often asserted, is due to the fact that the rush is cut green in summer and the reed dry in winter, and also to their having grown upon different soils. According to this opinion, what is reed on the salt marsh by Yarmouth, where there is a rich ooze soil, becomes rush farther inland, when it grows on the poor, boggy soil of the Broads. Botanically, the plaiting rush and one kind of reed belong to the same natural order ; the common reed, however, belongs to an entirely different order. To the ordinary observer the reed is easily distinguishable from both rush and sedge, whereas these two last, although belonging to different orders, have a general resemblance. All three are used to some extent in rural industries.

REEDS. There are two plants commonly known as reeds, both of which grow in marshes or shallow water, and are used for thatching. One, with round, hollow stems, belongs to the grass family, *Gramineae*, genus *Phragmites*, and is very common all over the world. Wide ditches and wet patches of ground full of this swaying, feathery-topped reed are a familiar sight in Norfolk and the Fen Country, particularly near Burwell, Ely, and Ramsey Heights in the latter district, where pieces of marsh land are especially kept for the reeds, which are cut every few years, the same plot never being cut in two successive years. The cutting takes place in winter, when the ' flag ' is off, and the reeds, being dry, do not need further treatment before use, as do the rushes. They are sold by the thousand bundles for thatching.

The other plant usually known as a reed, is the Fen Sedge, of the order *Cyperaceae*, genus *Cladium*, and has solid, angular stems. It used to be very common in the Fens, near Cambridge, before they were drained, and was used in that town for lighting fires and for thatch.[1] It still grows in great quantities in the undrained Wicken Sedge Fen, near Ely, which is one of the few pieces of natural fen now remaining.

The characteristic of both kinds of reed, so far as their use in industry is concerned, is that they have a hard, woody stem, which is not flexible, but jointed like that of the bamboo ; thus it cannot be used for plaiting, but makes an excellent thatch. It grows about six feet high, and when dry becomes very brittle and readily breaks at the joints.

Reed thatch is a very old form of roofing, in fact older than straw thatch ; it is used in the Fen District fairly extensively for barns and cottages, although straw thatch is perhaps more common nowadays, because it is cheaper, every farmer having his own supply of straw, whereas reeds must usually be bought. The greater amount of labour which goes to making a reed thatch also increases the cost, but a thatching of reeds lasts much longer than one of straw —' for a hundred years ', was the boast of one old fenman. It is made a foot or more thick, the reeds being put on in layers, their even ends receding up the roof, and tied with tarred string. There is a certain demand for reed thatching in districts far beyond the Fen Country, particularly for club-houses and summer-houses, which are often given an ornamental thatch, cut away in patterns along the roof-tree. A firm at Salhouse (near Wroxham Broad) sends thatchers, carrying with them their thatching of Norfolk reeds, as far afield as the Thames Valley and Cheshire.

Reeds are put to several other uses in Norfolk and the Fen Country. In a certain type of roofing, of which an example was seen on an old mill, and which is often found on farm buildings, reeds are laid beneath the tiles. The spars run in a lateral direction and the laths across them ; on the laths the reeds are laid, and on them the mortar and tiles. When the latter are laid without the reeds and mortar, they are said to be ' laid dry ', and the roof is apt to leak.

[1] *Flowers of the Field*, by the Rev. C. A. Johns.

Another common use for reeds is to build fences by standing them upright and tying them in place. They make a good wind screen, and many cottage gardens and yards, especially where pigs and other animals are kept, are surrounded by this sort of fence.

Reeds are also used in shipyards, being burnt under the keel of a ship when the workmen want to dry her quickly in order to hurry on with the repairing work. The reeds are sold to the shipyards by the fathom—a bundle of six feet in circumference, containing either five large bunches or six smaller ones. The price in 1923 was 1s. 6d. per fathom.

RUSHES. There are two distinct plants which go by the general name of ' rush' for industrial purposes. One, the Club Rush, belongs, like the Fen Sedge, to the order *Cyperaceae*, the botanical ' sedge family '; it is the genus *Scirpus lacustris*, and is green and usually leafless, with spongy, erect stems, cylindric at the base, and gradually tapering upwards to a height of ten or twelve feet. It is popularly known in many parts of the country as a bulrush, although to some people this name denotes the stiff ' poker rush ', which is the plant known to Norfolk plaiters as sedge, and is botanically a Reed Mace. This single example of varied nomenclature gives some idea of the great difficulty in distinguishing the different kinds of plants used in this group of industries. An old Norfolk man, when asked about the popular name of bulrush for the plaiting rush, quoted from the Bible, ' bending like a bulrush ', and pointed out that the characteristic of these rushes used for plaiting is that they are pliable, whereas that of the stiff ' poker ' kind, the sedges, is that they bend sharply and could not be plaited.

The Club Rush grows either in still or in running water, but is tougher, and therefore better for industrial purposes, when growing in deep, swiftly flowing rivers. It is cut green every two years, and is used for the seating of chairs and for plaiting into mats, hassocks, horse-collars, and baskets, and also in coopering. Great care must be taken in handling rushes, as they easily become bent in many places, and then look jaded and untidy when plaited.

These rushes are cut in Norfolk in Barton Broad, in Wroxham Broad, near Hoveton St. John, and elsewhere, and they also grow plentifully in the Bedford Ouse, the Nene, and the Cherwell. The Ouse rushes are reported to be the best of all. They are cut chiefly in the St. Ives and Pavenham districts, and in the Nene at Islip (near Thrapston,

Northants). Islip, in Oxfordshire, is also said to have been a great centre of rush-cutting at one time. The rushes near St. Ives are thought to be particularly good, and many people used to come here to cut them and send them to rush-plaiting industries at Islip (Northants), Norwich, and elsewhere. Because rushes are bulky, awkward things to transport, and also because a certain amount of labour is needed during a short season for cutting and drying them, industries sprang up by the river side for plaiting rushes and making up baskets, mats, and various other things. At Islip (Northants) and Pavenham (Beds.) these village industries were once particularly large, but they are now much diminished.

Club rushes also grow in the river Avon, near Leamington, but now they are cut here only by one man, who is building up a business for the making of rush-seated chairs and other hand-made furniture. Basket-makers in the neighbourhood used to cut a few for chair-seating, and for making rush-plait to be woven into wicker furniture, but they now seem to find it cheaper to buy imported rushes and ready-made rush-plait from the Birmingham dealers.

A Bridgwater firm making wicker chairs rents cutting rights for rushes in another part of the river Avon, near Tewkesbury. During the war this firm used a certain quantity of English rushes, the plaited rush from Belgium being difficult to obtain. Before the war only Belgian rush-plait was used in the Bridgwater district for furniture work, but in 1922 two Sussex basket-makers in different towns spoke of buying rush-plait from Somerset, so that it seems likely that the firm has continued to cut and plait English rushes, not only for local use, but also for sale.

At Norwich there is a factory for making up horse-collars, housemaids' kneelers, ' frail ' baskets, and other goods both of rush and of sedge. Apart from this, only five rush-workers were heard of in Norfolk, two at Stalham, two at Neatishead, and one at Hoveton St. John. The making of horse-collars was a great industry at Islip, and some plait is still supplied to makers there from Pavenham. This village and Islip are the chief centres of the industry in the East Midlands ; a cutter at Holywell (St. Ives) used to employ four or five men on rush-plaiting, but had given this up before the war. The Women's Institutes in Northamptonshire, Huntingdonshire, and Norfolk, as well as in Dorset and Hampshire, have taken up rush-work to some extent. Rushes used to be cut and harvested in Dorset, the smaller ones being used for workmen's baskets and the seating of chairs, and the larger ones sold to coopers, long before rush-work was developed here as an artistic craft by the Women's Institutes.

Though rushes are not so thickly grown in Essex as in Norfolk, there are certain lock-keepers along the canal near Chelmsford who will cut and dry rushes for any one who sends an order before the 1st of June. After that date, all that remain are cut, together with the weeds, to clear the canal, and allowed to drift down stream.

Another kind of rush, of which some use is made in industry, belongs to the botanical ' rush family ', *Juncaceae*, and is the plant which was at one time strewn on the floors of halls and churches in lieu of carpets ; it was also twisted into cordage, and made into wicks for tallow candles. It has a cylindrical stem, from one to three feet high, tapering to a point, with a brown, tufted flower and a white pith. The small rushes gathered from ditches by some Women's Institute members in Essex and Suffolk for plaiting seem to be a variety of this order. These rushes are also used sometimes in place of *Scirpus lacustris* for seating chairs.

SEDGE, though like the rush in appearance, belongs to the botanical order *Typhaceae*, or Reed Mace, and is not botanically a sedge, although it bears this name among the Norfolk workers. Elsewhere it is more commonly called a bulrush. Two varieties are used industrially, *Typha latifolia*, the Great Reed Mace, and *Typha angustifolia*, the Small or Narrow-leaved Reed Mace. It grows in stagnant water— ponds or marshes ; the flower is long and thick, of the heavy, brown ' poker ' or club variety. Rushes grow up straight from the roots, generally without any leaves, whereas sedge has leaves sheathed at the base. The large variety of Reed Mace is that chiefly used on the Broads, and it is taller, bigger, and coarser than the rush. This kind of sedge is in Norfolk sometimes called ' gladden ', although this name elsewhere is applied to the iris or flag. It has a long, brown thread running down the inside of the stem, and one of the old Fen men told how, in his childhood, he and others were made to remove this thread from the gladden and twist it ready for the sedge-workers to use as sewing thread for the horse-collars which they made. So many yards of it had to be twisted every day before the children were allowed to go out to play. To-day string is used.

Country people living near the Avon have another use for the sedge or ' poker rush ' which grows there, though this has never developed into an industry. They cut the heads and hang them up to dry ; the heads are then pulled apart and the vegetable down from inside them is used as stuffing for cushions.

Cutting and Drying, Plaiting and Making-up.

The industrial value of rushes depends largely upon their cutting and preparation. Only from experience can the rush-cutter learn to know the right moment for cutting, the time needed for drying, and the best way of sorting the rushes. No cultivation is needed, either for rushes, sedge, or reeds, but they should be cut every two years, or the quality deteriorates. Careless drying may seriously diminish the value of a crop, but even before the rushes are cut they may be spoilt by summer floods which cover them with mud and rubbish. On the other hand, if the season is very dry, with a great deal of sun, the rushes will be brittle and of little value.

There is some diversity of opinion as to the season when cutting should take place, but it is generally considered that rushes should be cut in July and sedge in September. One man begins his cutting on the longest day of the year, 21st June ; another waits until August, and others range in between these two extremes. Northamptonshire rushes are usually considered superior to those grown in Norfolk, and one reason given for the difference in quality is that the latter, being cut too late in the year, are coarse and stiff, and not so suitable for weaving as those from the Nene. If this is the case, it is clear that the better quality of rush can be produced in Norfolk, and a few experiments would prove whether the difference in quality is really due only to the date of cutting or to some peculiarity of soil or water in one of these districts. There is a great temptation to cut as late as possible, because then the rushes are bigger, and therefore fewer are required to make up the bundle. Those who favour late cutting claim that the rushes are then tougher, and that those cut in June are apt to be sappy.

Cutters on the Ouse go up the river in boats and wade into the water, cutting the rushes with a sharp blade on the end of a seven or eight foot pole ; half a scythe blade is generally used for the purpose. Reeds, since they grow in shallow water, can be cut easily with a hook on a short handle. Rushes must be cut below the surface of the water, as near to the roots as possible. They are brought out of the water into the boat by means of a drag and conveyed

down the river to the drying ground ; they must be washed
clean of mud and weeds before being dried.

The following description of cutting the variety of reed
known as Fen Sedge (*Cladium mariscus*), in Wicken Sedge
Fen, is given by Samuel H. Miller : ' After the reaping the
sedge is tied in bundles ; but there are no roads—perhaps
a horse never trod on the Fen—therefore the whole work
is done by hand labour. Two long poles are placed on the
ground, the bundles of sedge or litter are laid across these
poles till there is sufficient for two men to carry. One man
goes to the front between the poles, another to the rear,
and the load is carried just as Sedan chairs used to be. In
the distance these loads look like small stacks floating
among the sedge. Arrived at the lode side, the first man
walks up to the spot where the sedge barges are moored in
the lode (the rear man has to follow the lead as if blind-
folded) ; the load is dropped and the poles drawn from
under the bundles, and are then ready to be filled by another
load.' [1]

The method of drying rushes differs slightly according to
the district. Great care is needed as, if the rushes are too
dry, they shrivel, or if too green, they rot. In Pavenham
they are dried in the sun, being taken in when it rains, for
they become spotted and spoiled in colour if they get wet.
The drying takes about a month or six weeks, according to
the weather. The Essex lock-keeper ' lays them down like
hay ', and they lie there for a week or ten days, being covered
or brought in if it rains, as at Pavenham. The shorter time
taken in drying is probably due to the fact that here the
rushes are cut before the 1st June, and are therefore smaller.

Around St. Ives (Hunts.) it is considered that drying is
best done in the shade, as the sun bleaches the rushes. The
method here is to tie them tightly together by the thin
tips, the butt ends being spread out fanwise, and thus they
are laid in meadows to dry for ten days or a fortnight or
even longer. In the best weather they will dry in a week.
If dried as quickly as this they are green in colour, but
those dried more slowly are brown or yellow. Very beautiful
orange shades are seen in rushes which have been well dried
and stored for a year or two in a dry place.

Near the Broads the rushes are tied for drying into
bundles about a yard round at the base ; four of these
bundles are stood up together and their tops tied, and six
more outside them with their tops also tied. These ten are

[1] *Handbook to the Fenland*, 1890.

called a ' heap ', or in other districts a ' lump ', and each
of the ten is a ' shoe ', which measures about thirty-six
inches round the butt. They are left standing through all
weathers until dry ; rain only touches the outside ones, and
runs off them as off a thatch, and the wind, blowing through,
dries them. The rush-cutter must keep a look out and set
them up again if they are blown over by the wind. All
Norfolk cutters agree that rushes take about six weeks to
dry. The fact that they are left out in all weathers may
help to account for the inferior quality of Norfolk rushes.

The licence to cut rushes is usually a small item, but the
rent of land on which to dry the rushes is a heavy expense.
The land is badly needed at that time of the year, and
although only a narrow strip along the river bank is used,
the whole meadow, which may stretch back for a long way,
must be rented to keep it clear of animals which would
injure the rushes.

The basis of work for an old-fashioned rush-worker, and
by far the most difficult thing to make, was rush-plait. It
is made in different widths, the number of rushes used at
a time varying according to the width. The plait is attached,
whilst being woven, to a wooden bar or to nails on the wall,
about waist high. Skill is needed to insert each rush in
such a way as to get the whole strip, many yards long, even
in texture and strength. The width varies from three or
four inches to a foot in width, but one very heavy kind of
plait, made only by men, is a yard wide. One type of
' three plait ', that is to say, the ordinary three-strand
plaiting, is only about an inch in width, and was made in
great quantities by women when the rush industries
flourished. This is the plait used so often for the decoration of wicker furniture of a cheap quality. The yard-wide
plait made by men was also known as ' three plait ' ; sevens
and nines were other varieties, made from the smaller and
shorter rushes. These, like the three plait, were narrow
pieces, used chiefly by basket-makers for decoration. The
strips are woven in Pavenham in three textures : fine,
which is made in strips forty yards long, middle, and coarse,
both of which are woven in thirty-six yards lengths.

The wide strips of plaited rush are used sometimes as
matting for churches and bungalows, and as hangings for
the walls of harness rooms ; they also form the material
from which many other things are made, such as hassocks,
' frail ' baskets, and one kind of horse-collar.

The sedge horse-collar is entirely different from that made

of rush.   For the former the material is prepared by fraying
out the sedge for about a foot up from the butt end.   The
worker pulls it over a rough iron comb fastened to the edge
of a table, as if he were heckling hemp or flax, and it is thus
shredded into long silky streamers of a pale buff colour,
velvety soft to the touch.   The tops of the sedge are then
braided together and the frayed ends are wrapped around
a stuffing of odd pieces of rush or sedge to meet the braid
again, forming a soft lining to come next to the horse's neck.
A very heavy plait is then made, about three inches wide
and two thick, several sedges being used in each of the
three strands.   This is sewn all round the top of the collar
to give it strength, a short tail being left at the point by
which to hang it up.   The effect is very rough, but it is both
cheap and useful, serving for horses that cannot stand the
roughness of an ordinary collar.   Local farmers use these
collars for training colts and for ploughing.   Sedge is also
used sometimes for making the ridge of a thatch, which is
cut away in a pattern above the lower part of the thatch.

For the wide, thin rush-plait, very different from the
coarse, three-strand plait of sedge used on the collars, and
giving the effect of a woven fabric rather than that of
a horse's braided tail, the most frequent use in Norfolk is
for the workman's ' frail ' basket.   This is a heavy, strong
basket, tall and narrow, made in various sizes, of which one
of the largest is about six inches wide, two feet high, and
about two and a half feet long.   Whatever the size, the proportions are the same.   A narrow cover is held in place by
two handles, which pierce it, and which are covered with
a rough sort of leather.   Two or three narrow bands of
a thicker sort of plait run around the basket to give greater
strength and also to help to form the handles.   The name
of ' frail ' for this large, heavy basket, chiefly used by workmen to carry their dinner and tools in, is peculiar to Norfolk.
Dictionaries give the derivation as from Old French ' frayel ',
of doubtful origin, and define the word as meaning also
' a rush ', although this use of it was not found.

Housemaids' ' kneelers ' are also made of rush or of sedge.
The soft part of the sedge is frayed out and used thickly as
a lining to a round mat made of thick braids of rush or
sedge, with a rim about three inches high round three sides.

Rushes are largely used for seating chairs, and many
basket-makers do this work, but now generally use Dutch
rushes.   The work needs skill and care.   The back of the
chair seat is usually narrower than the front, but the same

number of rushes must cover each. Every rush must be put in its right place, and must be so manipulated that as the worker, working from the outside, nears the middle, the space between the rushes on each side is kept even and the sides of the work, originally inclining towards one another, become parallel. Amongst other users of rushes on a small scale, in addition to the basket-makers already referred to, who weave rush-plait into wicker-work, there are many handicraft workers, who make hats, baskets, and mats of rush-plait, and some who weave mats of rushes on a string warp. Coopers in all districts use the biggest rushes for any tub or barrel which has to be water-tight, such as wash-tubs or beer-barrels. These are 'bottomed' with rushes coiled round between the stave-heads and the boards which form the bottom of the barrel. The rushes are often put between each stave as well, to fill up the slight crevices. The ordinary jobbing cooper uses very few rushes ; one had had a bundle on hand for twenty years, though another used this amount each year. The latter gathers his own and dries them for a few days in the sun, but many buy from the regular rush cutters. The coopers at Burton-on-Trent use a great many, and a rush-cutter near St. Ives sends most of his crop to them.

Labour.

The simple, narrow three-plait which was made at Pavenham some years ago was very easy to plait, and was often done by boys and girls as well as by women. According to one estimate, a girl could plait about two hundred yards a day, for which she was paid 2s. Even in 1920 wages seem still to have been low in this district. A man working from 7 a.m. to 8.30 p.m. earned £2 a week. In Norwich, in 1923, the hours were from 9 a.m. to 6 p.m. Here the plaiters were all on piece work, and a man or a woman who was at all quick could earn from 30s. to 35s. a week. Of the nine-and-a-half inch plait, which is the kind used for horse-collars, a very good workman makes two feet in an hour. To make up a sedge collar takes the same workman two and a half hours. At one time the Norwich firm employed about thirty workers, both men and women, but trade in 1923 was so bad that they had only five or six. In the opinion of the foreman of this workshop women are apt to be best at the plaiting, as they have smaller, quicker fingers.

The question of apprenticeship in this interesting old

industry is an important one.   The work is light, but highly
skilled.   Unless the firm in Norwich can succeed in interesting young workers in rush-plaiting, the industry will certainly die out in that district.   Most of the independent
workers in Norfolk are old men, and few of them have
trained younger men to carry on the trade after them.   One
of them has six sons, of whom only one has taken up the
industry, and even he gives more than half his time to
a small holding, which interests him more than rush-work.
He himself has a son who, rather than take up rush-plaiting,
has become a labourer on a farm near by.   He craves an
open-air life, and the trouble with rush-work is that it is
not only difficult and poorly paid, but is also done under
rather uncomfortable conditions.   The rushes have to be
damped when they are to be worked up, and this makes
them unpleasant to handle in cold weather, whilst a fire
fills the room with steam.   Even in summer the work must
be done indoors, otherwise the rushes will dry too quickly.
With these small men, who are their own masters, the work
is always solitary, and young people are gregarious.   Only
in the Norwich workshop were people working together,
with the consequent cheerfulness of human society.   If any
scheme of apprenticeship is undertaken it will be here, and
the foreman would be an excellent man to carry out such
work.   He is both interested in the industry and ready to
impart his knowledge and skill to others.   Those who have
been taught by him speak highly of his capacity.   There is
an elderly man at Neatishead, who has now given up the
work, but who has taught many people in his time.   He
stated that simple plait-weaving, the first stage in rush-
work, takes some months to learn ;   many men are as bad
at the end of three months as at the beginning, but if a man
is likely ever to be a good rush-worker he ought to be
' getting on with it ' at the end of six months, and some,
who are very quick with their fingers, ' begin to see through
it ' by the end of six weeks or so.   The best pupil this man
ever had was an educated woman who was working on
a farm near by during the war.   She was dependent for her
livelihood on farm work, and learnt rush-plaiting in order
to provide herself with an additional source of income
during bad weather when farm workers are ' stood off '.
She has since found that it is possible to support herself all
the year round by this work, partly because she has more
talent for artistic and original work than have any of the old
Norfolk fenmen, and also because she is better able than they

are to judge what will please the modern buyer of decorative rush-work.

Marketing of Rushes, Sedge, and Reeds, and of Articles made from them.

The prices of rushes vary greatly, according to the season and the quality of the crop, and also from district to district, as do also the sizes of the bundles. In Northamptonshire, in 1922, the wholesale price was £12 10s. for a hundred bundles, a bundle being ' as big as a man can put both arms round ', and weighing from twelve to fourteen pounds. The pre-war price for a hundred bundles was £5, and in 1916 they sold for £20, that being a bad season in which rushes were very scarce. The price of Northamptonshire rushes as quoted in Norwich was from 3s. 6d. to 4s. a bolt in 1923, the bolt measuring forty inches round the butt. The Northamptonshire bolt, or bundle, is larger than the Norfolk one, and the rushes are superior in quality, besides being sold in a cleaner state, with less mud on them. A good price for the Norfolk rushes, in 1923, was £3 a hundred bolts ' green ' (not dried), and £4 a hundred ' weathered up ' (dried). This bolt is only thirty-six inches round the butt, but there are six score bolts in a ' hundred '. The pre-war price was 30s. a hundred, green.

Fine rushes for seating chairs were quoted at 5s. 6d. a bundle in 1922, while the Dutch product was 7s. 6d., being better and firmer. A chair could be seated for 4s. with English rushes, and for 5s. with Dutch rushes. These prices were given in Sussex, where rushes are not grown. The narrow rush-plait bought from Somerset for use in basket-making cost, at this time, 13s. 6d. for a thousand yard ' skein ', 1s. being added on to the price for railway carriage.

A Pavenham employer stated, in 1920, that it cost him £200 to buy the right of cutting rushes, to cut them, and prepare enough to keep four men busy during the winter. The four men used a thousand of the forty-inch bolts a year. This is probably an estimate based on the selling price of the rushes rather than on the actual cost to the cutter. The Norwich firm uses from two thousand to three thousand bolts of rushes in a year, the variation in quantity being due to the fact that in a dry season the rushes are smaller. The season of 1922 was a bad one for rushes, dry in May and June, and wet later on. They were not able to grow to any size early in the year through lack of water, and later they had no chance to dry properly.

Much of the simple three-plait from Pavenham used to be supplied to big firms in Leicester and elsewhere, who made it up into many different articles, but foreign plait has displaced it. The market for Pavenham rushes has for some time been steadily decreasing. Some years ago travellers used to call regularly and order workmen's baskets in quantities ranging from four dozen a month to six dozen a week, but by 1922 orders were coming only from the large firms who make the matting used in churches. At Islip a few baskets and mats were being made for local retail orders in 1923, and plait was sent from Pavenham to Islip for the horse-collars which were still being made here. The greatest demand for the Norfolk sedge collars comes from Wales, whither they are sent in large quantities for the pit ponies. They cost about 2s. 6d. each.

Other prices in 1923 were 3s. 6d. a square yard for matting and 7s. 10d. for a ' nest ' of four frails, twelve, fourteen, sixteen, and eighteen inches respectively in length, made of coarse plait. Nests of frails made of fine plait and measuring respectively ten, twelve, fourteen, and sixteen inches were the same price.

Prospects for the Rush and Sedge Industries.

At Pavenham about a hundred workers, men and women, boys and girls, were employed twenty or thirty years ago. The work done by the women and girls, the narrow three-plait, died out long before the war, but the more skilled work, the making of the heavier, wider plaits, lasted up to that date, and is still carried on to a certain extent. Even before the shortage of labour due to the war it had already diminished, owing chiefly to three causes. When the employment of children was prohibited, and boys and girls could no longer plait the ' sevens ' and ' nines ', this work became unprofitable, and so the inferior rushes, which were used in these plaits, became so much waste material and had to be burnt. There was also increasing difficulty, common to nearly all these rural crafts, of getting lads and men to learn the more skilled work and to undertake the heavy task of making the wide strips. Thirdly, the importation of very cheap Belgian plait reduced prices until very little profit could be made on the industry. Belgian ' seven ' and ' nine ' plait was sold for 10d. or 1s. per hundred yards, which was the cost of the labour for making it in England. The simple three-plait work was the first to die out owing to foreign competition. When 1s. 6d. per hundred yards

HORSE COLLARS

REED BED AT ELY

was paid for making it in Pavenham, it was being imported from Belgium at the price of 6*d.* per hundred yards.

From the neighbourhood of Islip came a story that during the war one of the Islip horse-collar makers, who had for some time found it cheaper to buy Belgian rush plait than to employ girls to plait the rushes that grow at his door, was held up for material when the Belgian imports ceased. He therefore applied to the Belgian Relief Committee, thinking that he might be able to employ the men whose work he had been buying. The committee regretted that they could not produce any rush-plaiters, because the work had only been done by convicts or inmates of reformatories. If this is true it helps to explain the extraordinary cheapness of Belgian plait in relation to the English product.

The opinion was expressed in Pavenham that only the invention of machinery for rush-plaiting would revive the industry here. There are three or four workers left, one of whom employs a few men to make plait for hassocks and workmen's bags; the others are small holders, who cut a few rushes, chiefly for their own use, and make wide strips of plait in their spare time. At Islip the industry at one time flourished in the form of numerous small workshops, in each of which two or three girls were employed to make the strips of plait, not very wide, and so not difficult to work on, which a man made up into horse-collars. About fifty years ago there are said to have been forty men at work here, but now there are only two, both of them growing old. The work was so poorly paid that no young men would learn it.

An attempt to revive the rush industry was found near Leamington, where the manager of a saw-mill was cutting rushes from the Avon for seating chairs and settees made in his mill. In only one other case were English rushes said to be actually cheaper than those imported from Belgium, but one or two Sussex basket-makers preferred the former for quality, and would gladly go on buying them if they could be obtained.

Though the opinion of the rush-*plaiters* about the future of their trade is not encouraging, the rush-*cutters*, who do not themselves make up the rushes, say that this part of the industry is profitable enough and on the increase. There seems to be a good demand for the heavy, coiled, rush mats, often decorated by the introduction of dyed rushes, which are suitable for country cottages, and which are sold chiefly in the few shops which cater expensively for individual and artistic tastes. If the making of these articles is taken up extensively by the Women's Institutes and other handicraft workers, it may open out new markets for the rush-cutter, many of whose old markets are now supplied by cheap foreign plait. From present conditions it seems unlikely that there is much future for the industry except as a handicraft practised by women who do not seek to earn their entire living by it. This aspect of the industry is dealt with more fully in a subsequent volume.[1]

The passing of the rush and sedge industries in the march of industrialism will be regretted by all those who value traditionary rural handicrafts and appreciate the picturesque aspects of country life. The district of the Broads and Fens is becoming more and more civilized, and the old marsh men fewer and harder to find. The rush-plaiters belong essentially to this fast-disappearing type.

The old men, however, are too conservative to learn the new types of decorative and varied rush work, such as are practised by the Women's Institutes workers, and which seem to constitute the only branch of the industry with a future. Doggedly and blindly they continue their old work in the face of the competition of cheaper foreign goods and the failure of the demand for many of the things they produce. The younger men, therefore, seeing rush work only as a difficult, unprofitable, and dying industry, refuse to learn it. When the old men can no longer find a market they give up the work altogether.

[1] See *The Rural Industries of England and Wales*, vol. iii, Decorative Crafts.

STRAW SKEPS

BEES nowadays would scorn to occupy one of those picturesque little domed huts—a straw skep—as a permanent residence ; this is regarded in the bee-world as the equivalent of a caravan, being used, in fact, only for the purpose of taking swarms or of sending bees by post. For a regular dwelling the modern bee demands a more elaborate house, the frame-hive, which may be built by a carpenter who is something of a bee-man or by the bee-man who is also a carpenter, but which more often comes from one of the big firms which manufacture all kinds of accessories used by the bee-keeper. The skep industry, therefore, is now a very small one, but, since nothing else seems to replace the skep for the special purposes for which it is still used, the demand should be steady. In fact, with the recovery of the bee-keeping industry from the Isle of Wight disease which ravaged it for so many years, a slight increase in the demand for skeps might be expected.

Skeps are made by a few individual workers who, in most cases, supply them wholesale to the big firms, such as those at Welwyn and Uxbridge, who make frame-hives, wax for combs, and other accessories, on a factory scale, and who supply the skeps to the ironmongers who retail them. Some makers may sell a few direct to bee-keepers or to local shops, but the supply seems to be almost entirely in the hands of the big firms, and many of the retailers do not know where the skeps are made. Occasionally skeps are seen for sale in a basket-maker's shop ; one in a Yorkshire town was said to make and sell skeps, and they were seen in a basket shop at Guildford, the owner of which said that, during the war, he bought them from the gipsies and now from several local makers. This was the only trace of skep-making as a gipsy industry and only one of the local makers was traced, an ex-service man who had learnt to make skeps as well as frame-hives and other accessories from an old bee-man in the neighbourhood. This maker, who lived in a Sussex village, sold his skeps to local bee-keepers as well as to the shop, and it seems likely that skep-making is carried on in the same way, as a subsidiary industry, by other bee-men in Sussex and

perhaps elsewhere. In the village of Earith, in the Fen
Country east of St. Ives (Hunts.), a chance encounter with a
man wheeling a barrow-load of skeps led to the discovery of a
maker here, who gave the information that his brother,
living in the village of Willingham, a few miles away, also
made skeps. These were not bee-men, but had other occupations connected with farming. They sold their skeps to
one of the large firms. It is probable that skep-makers who
depend mainly on some other source of livelihood are to be
found in other parts of England, but the centre of the
industry seems to be in the straw-plaiting district of Hertfordshire, where there are makers at Hitchin and in the
village of Lilley, near Luton. The maker at Lilley also keeps
a village shop and deals in coal, but the Hitchin skep-makers
have no other occupation. One of them was formerly a
straw-plaiter. These two industries were probably closely
connected ; the farmers here have, for generations, been
accustomed at threshing time to set aside a certain amount
of wheat straw for use in both industries, chopping off the
heads to be threshed. Thus skep-makers here have no
difficulty in obtaining unthreshed straw, but in the Fens,
where this is not a local custom, they sometimes find difficulty in getting it. One of the skep-makers here is a
threshing-machine ' feeder ', and so generally manages to
bargain with the farmers at threshing time to let him have
some straw before it goes into the machine ; sometimes his
supply runs short and he then has to use threshed straw,
which, being cracked and bent, is more difficult to work
and does not look so well when made up.

All the skep-makers met with were individual workers
without employees. The season when skeps are most in use
is from May to the end of July, but, owing to the system by
which the makers sell to wholesale dealers, the industry is
not a seasonal one, although it would be so in cases where the
makers sell their skeps direct to the bee-keepers.

The Making of Skeps.

The skep-maker's peculiar skill consists chiefly in keeping
the regular shape of the skep. The straw is taken in handfuls
and twisted into a rope. The ' flag ' must be stripped off, as
these dark brown, leafy pieces spoil the appearance of the
skep. A disk of wood with a hole in the centre is the foundation, round which the straw rope is coiled, and to which
the first coil is nailed. As the work proceeds, strips of split
cane or willow are used to bind the coils, being threaded or

' stitched ' alternately over and under a coil, radiating outwards. Briars (the long shoots of blackberry bushes), or
tarred string can also be used for stitching the skeps, but are
considered rather inferior substitutes. When willow is used,
Spaniards, peeled, are the rods preferred. They are soaked
and split with a boxwood cleave into four ' skeins ', which
are then drawn through the ' shaver '. This is a steel plate,
about three inches by five inches, screwed on to a wooden
block ; across the centre is fixed a blunt-edged blade, the
edge slanting towards the surface of the plate and capable of
adjustment by a screw. Each skein is drawn through
between the blade and the plate, the pith thus being scraped
out and the skein rendered supple. It is clear that the
preparation of these willow skeins for stitching the skeps adds
greatly to the skep-maker's work, and that skeps stitched
with tarred string can be made far more quickly. Moreover,
if cane or willow is used, the cost of this is the most expensive
item amongst the material, cane costing 1s. per lb. and willow
rather less. The cost of the straw is small.

Skep-making must be carried on in a shed or outhouse,
as the straw makes a great deal of litter, especially when the
flag is being stripped off. The skep is held between the
maker's knees as he works and this, as one man pointed
out, ' comes hard on the trousers '.

Two kinds of skeps are made, the Skep proper, with its
wooden disk on the top; and the Dome, or Super, without the
disk and of a smaller size, which is used to stand on top of the
skep. The estimate of the time taken to make a skep varies
from two hours for a single one to ten skeps made in a day.
The latter is probably the minimum time and would only be
possible when the skeins are split beforehand or when string
is used. The former was the estimate of an old man, who
perhaps works slowly, and he was probably including in the
time the splitting of the cane which he uses.

The Selling of Skeps.

The wholesale price paid to skep-makers was at the rate
of 1s. 6d. a skep in 1921, but in 1922 had been reduced to
1s. or 1s 2d. a skep, the skeps being sold by the dozen. Two
of the Hertfordshire makers had, in protest against this
reduction, refused to sell their skeps at less than 1s. 4d. each
wholesale, maintaining that at any lower price they could not
make a profit. This seemed to be a slight exaggeration,
since another maker, who was selling them for 1s. and 1s. 2d.
each, and supers at 10d. each, considered the industry a

profitable one.   The striking point about the prices, however, is that at this time the skeps were retailed at 3*s*. 6*d*. each, providing a gross profit of from 200 to 250 per cent. for the middleman and the retailer between them, the supers being sold at 2*s*. each, representing a gross profit of 140 per cent. These were the prices in several shops and in the retail catalogue of the firm to which the Hertfordshire makers sold their skeps, from which the shops bought them.   Information was obtained that the price to the makers who supplied the Guildford shop was 2*s*. 6*d*. for a skep and that it had been from 3*s*. 3*d*. to 3*s*. 6*d*. during the war, whilst the pre-war *retail* price was only 1*s*. 3*d*.   At the same time a Sussex bee-man stated that he sold his skeps retail for 4*s*. 3*d*.   It was probably a very justifiable indignation at the discrepancy between wholesale and retail prices, rather than any real conviction that their work was seriously underpaid, that caused the Hertfordshire makers to go on strike.

The position seems to be that each of the few firms who deal in skeps has its own makers who supply all it needs, and, through the fact that these firms also sell all kinds of bee appliances, they have almost complete control of the market, which must always be a strictly limited one.   The few skep-makers who are also bee-men, making bee-food, hives, &c., and giving expert advice on bees, are by this means brought into touch with customers for the skeps and do not meet with any serious competition.   But the other makers, isolated and unorganized, are completely in the dealers' hands and must accept whatever price is quoted them.

PART II. FACTORIES IN RURAL DISTRICTS AND OUTWORK FOR FACTORIES

CHAPTER I

INTRODUCTORY

As a general rule factory industries have not been included in this survey, but there are some which are directly connected with rural problems and these are considered under three main headings.

1. There are factories whose raw material is some agricultural product, bulky and expensive to transport and often requiring immediate treatment, which is therefore more conveniently dealt with on the spot. For example, the preparation for the market of flax, peat, and sugar-beet is now largely carried on in factories, on a fairly large scale and chiefly by machinery, the factories being situated in the midst of the districts where these things are produced. In the cider- and cheese-making industries we have examples of the process of change from small scale production to large. These things are still often made on the farm, and sometimes only in sufficient quantities to supply the farmer's family. In some districts, however, particularly where a noted variety of cider or cheese is made, there is a tendency for them to develop into factory trades. Factory production in these industries has been described in most cases by specialist writers, and the only industry in this group which is dealt with here is the ancient one of peat-cutting.

There is another group of factories, ranging from small workshops to places of considerable size, with a miscellaneous output, the work of which is not described under any of the rural industries treated separately, and which are considered here in two main sections.

2. Many of the factories situated in rural districts are more closely connected, as regards processes and organization, with the large factories of the industrial areas, being really only country cousins of the latter, not separate industries but branches of the same industry. They are, however, of a certain importance from the point of view of rural economics

because the labour employed is drawn from the rural population and, in fact, the existence of this labour supply may, in some cases, have determined their situation. This is particularly so in the case of those factories which rely largely upon outwork, and these are grouped together in a separate chapter (Outwork for Factories). The outworker, who is to be found both in the industrialized and almost suburban villages of the Midlands and also in some of the most rural and isolated hamlets of Oxfordshire, Worcestershire, and the south-western counties, is really the modern representative of the cottage craftsman or craftswoman of more than a century ago. He has fallen, however, from his position as an independent worker to the ranks of the most poorly paid factory employee.

Outworkers are employed by factories to carry out in their own homes some process of manufacture, usually one requiring only the simplest of tools and no very great skill. The work may be fetched by the outworkers from the factories and taken back when finished, but, nowadays, is more often taken to them in motor-vans, which call for it again in due time. The process done by the outworker is usually only one small stage in the manufacture of the article and one which cannot economically be carried out by machinery. The work is paid for by piece-rates on completion, and the payment is usually on a low level, because the worker is often some one who is unable, through domestic circumstances or physical inability, to go out to regular work, and is therefore in a helpless position in the labour market. Although some outworkers are, in a sense, skilled craftsmen, they are often entirely dependent on the particular factory for which they work, especially when this is an isolated one in a rural district.

3. The factories in the third group (Some Small Rural Factories) are included in this survey because they are situated in rural areas and are therefore interesting from the point of view of their relation to local conditions and to the more truly rural industries. There are many factors which have led to their foundation or survival in agricultural areas. Some factories which depend to some extent on the labour of village outworkers are themselves situated in villages and country towns and draw their indoor workers also from the rural neighbourhood. Some are relics of the early days of industrialism, before the great industries came to be concentrated in large towns and in the neighbourhood of the coal-fields. Generally the isolated country factory was soon

beaten in competition with a rival in the industrial Midlands or North, but occasionally, through some freak of fortune, or perhaps because it retained control of some small but steady local market, whose needs it could meet exactly, the small factory survived. This is especially so in the south-west of England, the district most remote from any industrial area.

There are also to be found a variety of curious little workshop industries, hardly coming under the heading of ' factories ', but treated in this chapter because they do not belong to any of the main rural industries and are more or less accidentally situated in the country.

In rural districts there are often to be found water-mills which have served for two or three different purposes as industries developed and migrated ; thus in the Yorkshire Dales many a spinning-mill was converted into a bobbin turnery when spinning became a process to be carried on by highly elaborate machinery, and now, again, the bobbin industry is migrating to larger factories in the lowlands, water-power being no longer sufficient for its needs. A blouse factory was found housed in an old flax-dressing mill in a village on the Plain of York. In the south-west these changes are common ; the woollen and flax, tanning and boot-making industries flourished here and, indeed, still survive to some extent. In one mill at Crediton boot-making followed weaving, and has now given place to sweet and lozenge-making. An Ottery mill where cloth was once woven has since been used for silk manufacture and blouse-making, and it is now the home of three industries, mineral waters, paper bags, and collars, each on a separate floor, but all deriving their power from the same water-wheel.

The presence of even a small mill in a village or country town gives rise in the course of time to an ' industrial ' population ; the custom for the girls to go to work in the factory rather than on the land or in domestic service becomes traditional, and the force of traditional custom is strong ; therefore when one industry dies out, often through the competition of a larger kindred industry in the Midlands or North, the existence of the empty mill and the idle workers often leads to the foundation of some new industry to utilize them.

In the south-west of England it is less easy than in the Midlands to draw the labour for a town factory from the surrounding country districts. Railway and motor-bus transport is less well developed, villages are more remote, and the rough, hilly roads present difficulties which are

discouraging to those who might cycle in to work. Therefore, if the village labour is to be utilized, the factories must
be set up in the villages, or else the outwork system must
be developed, as it is to a great extent in this part of England.
In country districts where there is a considerable ' residen-
tial ' population of the wealthier classes, as in Sussex, Surrey,
and Hants, these small rural factories are not found, for there
is plenty of work as domestic servants, gardeners, &c., for
any of the population not engaged in farming. In market-
gardening, fruit- and hop-growing areas also there is enough
additional occupation, even if it is only seasonal, to enable
the women and girls of the farm-labourer's family to contribute their quota to the family income without seeking work
in factories. Thus, these ' rural factories ' are to be found for
the most part in the remoter rural districts where, except for
agriculture, and that not of a kind which calls for much
seasonal labour, there is little or no other occupation.

In the Midlands, on the fringes of the industrial areas,
factory life also touches the agricultural population very
nearly, but here the conditions are different. In Nottinghamshire, for example, it seems impossible to find any
village so far away from a factory town that no one goes
there daily to work, either by cycle, motor-bus, or train.
Roads and transport services are good in order to supply
the needs of the industrial towns. In many of the Midland
counties, if the village does not go to the factory the factory
comes to the village. In Northants the boot-making
industry has pushed out its tentacles into many a rural
village, setting up its factories and colonies of workmen's
dwellings. The case here is rather different from that of the
rural factory in Somerset or Devon. The latter is remote
from the main centres of the industry and must organize its
supplies of raw material and marketing of goods on its own
lines. It often has an opportunity of gaining control over
the market in its own district, and may cater specially for the
individual needs of this district and supply goods direct to the
retailers or even retail to private customers. The boot
factory in a Northamptonshire village lacks this advantage,
since the larger factories of Northampton and Welling-
borough are so near at hand, but it has the greater advantage of being able to avail itself of the organized supply of
fuel and raw material which has been called forth by the
demands of an industrial centre. In fact, these village
factories in the Midlands seem to be but grim precursors of
the main body of industrialism which is steadily spreading

and blackening the face of the country-side. The little rural
factories of the West Country are, on the other hand, more
in the nature of isolated phenomena, with little prospect of
any considerable extension. It is these latter which are
considered in the chapter on small rural factories, since they
affect what are otherwise purely rural districts. They are
many and various and have not been investigated exhaus-
tively, but a brief survey of some typical examples, together
with some account of a few curious and unusual specimens,
may serve to give some idea of their organization, their
influence on the country-side, and their future prospects.

The outwork system has many ramifications and is sometimes difficult to trace, factories being, in certain cases,
unwilling to give information concerning their outworkers.
The chief industries dependent upon outwork, such as
gloving, hosiery, and net mending, are well known, but a
great many other industries employ outworkers, sometimes
only a dozen or less, on some curious little process, and where
the factory is one which does not come ordinarily within the
scope of this survey this branch of its activities is easily over-
looked. Outwork in some seventeen different industries, in
both rural and industrial areas, has been investigated, and
these examples should serve to give a general picture of the
whole system, even though some varieties of outwork may
have been passed over.

CHAPTER II

THE PEAT INDUSTRY

The peat industry furnishes an example of the local manufacture of agricultural products. Peat occurs in a few well-defined districts.

The peat beds of Somerset lie to the north of the Polden Hills, between Glastonbury and Bridgwater, and peat or turf is cut in the parishes of Ashcott, Shapwick, Catcott, Burtle, Edington, Meare, and Godney. In some places the peat is sixteen feet deep and is of two kinds, brown above and black beneath. Black peat is found below brown on the Dartmoor peat-setts and on the Cumberland peat mosses, where the latter kind is usually known as ' white moss '. The process of formation is similar to that of the formation of coal. The brown peat which lies uppermost was formed, it is said, by the gradual decay of fibrous grass and weeds. In a field that is not cut or grazed the old grass gradually decays while the new grass forms above it. This brown peat, or white moss, is not of much use for fuel, as it is too quickly consumed, but it is used for horse litter and is said to make excellent manure. The top layer of all is so full of seeds as to be useless ; it is thrown back into the cut area and the seeds produce rank vegetation.

The Somerset peat beds are very picturesque, with their luxuriant growth of marsh flowers, set off by the dark ' cocks ' or ' ruckles ' of peat, with the low line of the blue Mendips as a background. According to a rough estimate there are over a thousand acres of peat still uncut in this district. The land is chiefly waste, but in process of cutting some of it comes under cultivation. It is too liable to flood in winter to be of use for arable farming, but gives excellent summer grazing. The dwellers on the edge are mostly small proprietors of land and cottages.

Most of the peat is worked by small men, but there are one or two big firms in the district ; the biggest of them manufactures briquettes at Highbridge and moss litter at Ashcott.

There are a number of small peat moss mills which for fifty years have worked the peat deposits on Crowle Moors on the boundary of Yorkshire and Lincolnshire. Whixall

SOMERSET PEAT CUTTERS

PEAT MUMPS

Moss, a peat bed near Whitchurch in Shropshire, resembles that between Bridgwater and Glastonbury, and the conditions of work are much the same. There is the usual white moss above and black below, and about six feet below the surface of the land there is a wet peaty substance which does not cling together. About six feet below that again is solid clay. In some parts the peat is shallower than this and there is but little of the valuable black variety. In working, the top weedy soil is thrown back on to the wet under-peat where the solid substance has been removed. The bottom layer of black peat is very solid and carboniferous and is called ' chatty '. Foxfield Moss and Rakes Moss are two large peat beds near Broughton-in-Furness. Peat has been cut here for many generations by the cottagers, as fuel for themselves, and certain cutting rights go with each farm. As a rule a tenant has not the right to turn cattle out upon the moss, but he can cut peat for himself and hire out to others the right to cut. Very little peat is sent away from here as fuel, but a company at Broughton disintegrates the white moss for horse litter. It was once fairly large and important, but now only two employees remain.

Another large moss, at Gretna Green, is rented from the Netherby estate by a company, which also works a peat moss at Blackrod in Lancashire, near Bolton, and others in Scotland. They treat the white moss for horse litter and do not deal in fuel. The company at Gretna has worked one thousand and forty acres for just over twenty years without exhausting half the area. They only dig three or four feet, to the point where the black moss, which is of no use to them, begins. The black moss which has been left is cut and used by the villagers for fuel.

Cutting begins each year as soon as the frosts are over, if it is not too wet to work the beds. In Somerset two men work together and can cut an acre in about three days if the weather is dry. As many as three crops can sometimes be taken in a dry year, the second being cut about June. One man cuts the blocks, or ' mumps ' as they are called in Somerset, while the other carries them off to be laid on their sides to dry. The ' mumps ', when a little drier, are cut into three turves each. Each mump measures 8 in. × 8 in. × 10 in. In Shropshire the peat is cut in cakes the size of the spade, these being then divided into three slabs and put on the surface to dry. They are built into low loose walls, called ' windrows ', instead of being ' hiled ', as in Somerset. If they do not dry enough like this they are then put into cocks, like the Somerset ruckles, and afterwards stacked. Some summers in the North are so wet that the peat does not get dried at all. The Gretna firm which crushes white moss for horse litter, cuts, stacks, and dries it all the year round, but white moss is much more porous than black and does not hold wet to the same extent.

After cutting there are two further processes, known in Somerset as ' hiling ' and ' ruckling '. The turf, when cut, is laid flat on the ground and then built into heaps of twelve, like card houses, so that the air can get to every side. These are called ' hiles ', and are probably similar in structure to the walls built on Crowle Moors. When fairly dry the peat in Somerset is ' ruckled ', or gathered into heaps, the ' pyramids ' of Crowle Moors. These are built into dome-shaped stacks, about five feet broad at the bottom and as high as the ' ruckler ' can conveniently reach. The outer walls are built honeycomb fashion, with air spaces between each turf, and the rest of the turves are heaped loosely inside. The peat can remain in ruckles indefinitely, but when thoroughly dry it is stacked, to protect it from wet and frost. If the frost is allowed to penetrate the peat crumbles. Where there is a factory for making peat moss litter the peat, after drying, is brought in and crushed. It is then compressed and sent away in crates of one hundredweight each.

Peat beds in Somerset have to be pumped in winter to keep down the water level. In 1921 it was estimated that there were about fourteen hundred men employed in the industry in Somerset. The biggest company had about seventy workers, two-thirds of whom were men. The beds here are largely worked by independent men, who rent a piece of land for a few years and cut the turf, and there were about one hundred men working beds in this way in the neighbourhood of Meare, Ashcott, Shapwick, Burtle, and Edington. The land from which the turf has been cut is also of a certain amount of use. One firm allows each man to have a piece of it rent free for three years to clean and crop with potatoes. The rent for the peat beds before the war was £5 per acre, and in 1921 it had risen to £10 an acre.

On Crowle Moors the industry is on a much smaller scale ; the largest of the peat moss mills employs ten men as a rule, another, three or four, and several smaller ones are worked by one or two men only.

In Somerset children are employed in their spare time to turn over the mumps, so that their under surface shall dry, and in 1921 they were paid 10s. an acre. Hiling is sometimes done by children and both this and ruckling are done by women. The peat has constantly to be turned about in the hiles in a wet season. Women were getting 35s. a week in Somerset in 1921, working from eight a.m. to four p.m. with about an hour off. Women are also employed on Crowle Moors to carry the blocks of peat and pile them into walls, pyramids, and stacks.

In 1921 the payment for cutting was at the rate of 9s. a ' road ', this being the number of slabs of peat sufficient to cover a piece of ground eight yards square. A man can dig a road and a quarter in a day. Another estimate for the same date and district (Somerset) was 15s. a day for cutting. Turf-cutting is said to be very heavy work and seven hours a day is considered long enough at it. Many cutters do not care to be employed on day work if they can earn enough by cutting their own peat beds. The work starts in March and goes on till September ; there is no work on the beds in winter.

In Cumberland a company formed for the purpose of making peat moss litter rents a large moss for a number of years. The first two or three years are spent in draining it and building the factory and not until after that do the profits begin. Cutting rights for individuals usually go with farms and cottages in this district.

In Somerset it is the custom for peat beds to be let for a period of ten years, during which time they are cleared of turf. Men often rent small beds which they work with the help of their families, or, sometimes, of neighbours. On Whixall Moss in Shropshire beds are rented for a year ; the men spend the summer in cutting and the winter in hawking the peat. This is the older method of marketing it for fuel. The women in Somerset are still to be seen driving into the towns in little carts built with high rails to hold the turves. The men used to do this, but recently the larger and more distant demand has enabled them to send it off in greater quantities by rail.

The biggest of the small firms in Somerset cuts two hundred and fifty truck-loads in one year and others from ten to forty. Seventy-five of the small businesses averaged about thirty-five truck-loads each in their output during the season 1919 to 1920. About four thousand five hundred and seventy-one tons were sent away from Shapwick station in 1919. The trucks are supposed to hold five thousand turves each, but the number varies, some men claiming that it is difficult to pack as many as four thousand turves into one truck.

About two thousand go to a ton and two tons to a truck. In 1921 the high freights were mentioned as a heavy charge on the industry, being more than double those of a few years before.

The price of peat fluctuates and seems to be open to private agreement to some extent. A pre-war price was £2 10s. a truck ; during the war it rose as high as £15 and in 1921 £8 was paid for a truck-load of black peat and £5 for brown. During the coal strike peat fetched as much as from 18s. 6d. to £1 a thousand turves. Single turves, which were six a penny before the war, were at that time sold in Bridgwater and Glastonbury at 1d. each. The pre-war price of moss litter was 20s. a ton. It rose considerably during the war and fell again to 55s. a ton in 1921.

Attempts have been made to start a co-operative society amongst the Somerset peat-cutters, but these have not met with success. Peat-cutting is not considered unhealthy work, the open-air life in some cases even counteracting the bad effects of poor houses, a number of which are on the ' droves ' across the marsh, on very spongy ground. The work was certainly underpaid before the war, and since the war-time prosperity of the trade, distinct improvement has been recorded in the health of the children. However, even now a living cannot be made from peat-cutting unless the whole family works, and, as with other employments, such as outwork, when the woman has to be earning money as well as looking after the house, the latter is apt to be neglected. Another drawback to the industry is the lack of work for the men in wet weather.

The increased use of motors has made a marked difference in the quantity of crushed peat needed for horse litter. This sort of bedding is not often used for cattle as most farmers grow enough straw for this purpose.

By-products of Peat. Experiments which have been made from time to time with the object of developing by-products from peat have always failed. There seems to be an insurmountable difficulty in removing surplus moisture.

PEAT RUCKLES

DELIVERING THEIR PRODUCT

CHAPTER III

OUTWORK FOR FACTORIES

OUTWORK is chiefly done by women. In remote rural districts it takes the place of factory work, absorbing the labour of employable women and girls of all ages, who might work within the factory itself if it were not too far away. In the industrial districts of the Midlands, on the other hand, where there are few villages which are not within reach of a factory, the outworkers are, for the most part, married women who have formerly been indoor factory hands, but who are now unable to leave their homes to go to work ; they have become in their turn the mothers of the new generation of factory labour. Outwork is done in many different kinds of industries, but one essential condition is that the materials for it should be light and small, and easy to transport ; otherwise the cost of taking them to the home workers and collecting them again would be prohibitive.

Distribution.

The hosiery industry, which flourishes in the counties of Nottingham, Leicester, Derby, and Warwick, provides a great deal of outwork on various processes. These are usually connected with the finishing by hand of machine-made garments. The most important is ' cheverning ', (pronounced with soft ' ch '), or embroidering clocks on stockings. The name is a corruption of an old word ' chevroning ', applied to embroidery in a V-shaped pattern. This work is done in nearly every cottage for several miles round Belper and in many other small places. Seaming and toeing (the finishing of the seams and toes of stockings), and chenilling (putting spots on veils), are other processes performed by outwork in the villages between Leicester and Nottingham, and between Derby and Belper. Grisewold work (knitting socks on hand machines), is also done as outwork in this district. It has been stated that hosiery outwork is not carried on more than two miles away from the factory which gives out the work, but chenilling, at least, was found at Long Clawson (Leics.), twelve miles from the factory in Nottingham.

The hand-frame knitting industry used to flourish in the neighbourhood of Nottingham and Belper and is still to be found within a radius of ten miles of the former and about three of the latter, in the villages of Arnold, Calverton, Lambley, Burton Joyce, and others near Nottingham. By merely walking through a village, the practice of hand-frame knitting is disclosed. Cottages are to be seen in which the upper stories are pierced with the many long windows characteristic of a weaving district, for the frame needs as much light as a loom, and from some of them comes the unmistakable long, heavy, click, click, of the frame knitter, each click, with a slight pause following it, signifying that another row of stitches has been added to the garment. Underclothes of various sorts are made on these machines, chiefly men's pants and vests and women's combinations, as well as silk and elastic bandages for surgical use.

At Belper, eight miles from Derby up the valley of the Derwent, another aspect of the hand-frame knitting industry was to be found. Although situated in the country, this is an industrial rather than an agricultural district ; the whole valley is studded with factories and the stream is harnessed to them. In Belper itself there is at least one factory for making woven silk undergarments, and special orders received for stockings or underwear of a particularly fine quality are given out to be made up on hand-frame knitting machines in the cottages round about.

The Nottingham lace factories provide outwork for many villages round about the town, the work done by hand being net mending, or repairing the flaws left by the machines. The threads that break and ravel have to be darned in, so that no sign of any flaw appears. Other processes done by outwork are scallopping, clipping, drawing, and jennying, this last consisting of winding lace on to a little wooden ' jenny ', or frame, ready for sale. The manufacture of net for lace curtains, mosquito netting, and dress material, is as old in Devon and Somerset as in Nottingham, and the factories at Tiverton, Barnstaple, Chard, and Chard Junction give out similar work to be done in the cottages. In Devon this work is done in the bobbin lace districts, where the women are skilled with their hands, although the processes are quite different. Similarly, some outwork known as ' bead work ' is done in Coggershall (Essex), where many of the women also make tambour lace, bead-work being simply a variant of this done in a much coarser style. It consists of crocheting fine silk braid on to machine-made net, which is used as trimming for hats. Being coarser it is easier and quicker work than the lace-making, but doubtless the presence of the latter in the districts gave rise to the bead-work, owing to the similarity of process.

Other sorts of outwork in the south-western counties are provided both by tooth-brush and by collar factories. There are two of the former at Axminster and one at Nummer, a small village near Chard. The brushes are taken home by the men who work in the factories to be bristled by their families; they are also carried to many villages within a radius of about ten miles from both places by motors, which collect and distribute the work once a week. There are a number of home workers at Ottery St. Mary, where there was at one time a branch factory. The outwork for the collar factories takes the form of machining round the edges of the collars, and it is given out from factories in both Devon and Dorset, an agent distributing and collecting the work. The enormous industry of making fishing-nets by outwork in and around Bridport and Lowestoft has been described in another volume.[1]

Some hand-sewing of boots is done as outwork by men in Northamptonshire for the numerous boot factories there. The ready-made clothing factories in this county used to give out button-holing and finishing work, but not only is this being done increasingly by machines within the factory, but the number of factories of this type has diminished in this district within the last few years.

In the villages around Luton and St. Albans, the centres of the straw hat industry, a certain amout of outwork is done, women stitching up the straw plait into hats by means of treadle sewing-machines. These outworkers are generally women who have formerly worked in the factories. The hat-making industry here owed its existence in the first place to the excellent quality of the wheaten straw grown in Hertford-shire, and straw-plaiting used to be an extensive cottage industry in this district. In 1871 there were thirty thousand plaiters, but by 1907 only a few hundreds remained and probably the number now is well under one hundred. Old women tell how straw-plaiting and lace-making were both practised by the same workers, who carried on the one or the other according to the demand of the moment. At that time straw-plaiting was not done as outwork but as an independent industry, as lace-making still is, by workers who took their plait into the nearest plait market for sale. As the demand for English straw plait decreased, the work came to

[1] Vol. i, *Timber and Underwood Industries and Some Village Workshops,* chap. iv, Ropes, Nets and Halters.

be done only to the order of dealers, who supplied the straw to ensure evenness of quality. Most of the plait now used in the hat factories is made abroad, but the plaiting industry has survived as outwork in a few villages easily accessible from Luton.   There is one Luton dealer who supplies manu- facturers with English plait when it is needed for special pur- poses, such as ' boaters ' for certain schools and colleges, and he drives round in a pony cart, giving out straw in these villages and collecting the finished work.   Thirty years ago there were still many straw-plaiters in villages as far north as Houghton Conquest, near Ampthill (Beds.), and westward as far as Stanbridge, near Leighton Buzzard.   Now the industry centres in Offley, five miles from Luton, where most of the married women of middle age and over are straw- plaiters.   In several other villages in the neighbourhood such as Pirton, Meppershall, and Shillingworth, there are a few plaiters, generally people who have migrated from Offley. At one time this industry extended into Essex, and was carried on extensively around Saffron Walden and Halstead. It has almost completely died out here, and in 1923 only one woman could be found who still practised the craft, and she was not an outworker.

In a group of industrial villages between Coventry and Nuneaton there is still some survival of the once famous industry of weaving ribbons on hand looms, which centred in Coventry and dates from long before the introduction of power looms.   Forty years ago hand loom ribbon-weavers were still fairly numerous, both in Coventry and in many surrounding villages.   In the poorer streets of Coventry the same feature which is seen in the villages around Notting- ham is noticeable ; many of the houses have very long windows in the upper stories, having been specially built to give light to the weavers.   The same windows are found in many old cottages in the villages within half a dozen miles of Coventry and Nuneaton, though now they are sometimes partially blocked.   In the suburbs of Coventry, especially the Foleshill district, there are numerous big, high buildings with immense windows in the top story (usually the third) ; they indicate that ribbon-weaving, besides being a cottage industry, was carried on by groups of weavers in small factories.   These big, well-lighted upper rooms were called ' top shops ', and a hand-loom stood at each window.   The buildings are now tenement dwellings, and the upper rooms, being too big to be comfortably inhabited, are often used only as attics.   Ribbon-weaving is still carried on in Bulkington, between Coventry and Nuneaton, in the adjacent village of Barnacle and in Chilvers Coton, a mile from Nuneaton. Possibly there are still a few ribbon-weavers in Coventry itself.

Outwork on weaving—but, in this case, of piece materials and not of ribbons—is found also on the borders of Suffolk and Essex. Over a hundred years ago some of the Spital-fields weavers came to Sudbury, in Suffolk, and others to Haverhill and Braintree. The large buildings with upper stories full of long windows, which are characteristic of all weaving districts, are also noticeable in these towns, and here the weaving still goes on steadily behind them. Though silk-weaving is chiefly done by power looms, and even the greater part of that which is done by hand is performed inside the factory, a certain amount still survives as outwork. The finest qualities of both silk and velvet, such as that used for coronation robes and royal weddings, are made on the hand looms inside the factory, but at Sudbury two old men weave velvet, chiefly for furniture, in their own homes, and in Haverhill there are a number of outworkers who weave umbrella silk. One or two of the latter work in their homes, but there are also two small workshops in which two and five men work respectively, being employed by London firms.

Though not rural in character, a curious little industry deserves mention, as analagous to outwork in conditions. In the heart of industrial Nottingham lives an old shuttlecock-maker and his family. This is the third generation which has carried on the trade, and the younger members of the family are being brought up to it. The work is not given out by a factory, this group of family workers providing their own materials and selling the work to shops and dealers, just as straw plait used to be made and sold, and as lace still is. The conditions under which the work is done are extremely unhealthy, and all the members of the family, young and old, look as though they had suffered all their lives from the worst results of sweated labour. At the opposite end of the scale is the doll industry of Braxted, near Witham in Essex. Started during the war by local women to give employment to the wives and daughters of soldiers, it has been a success from the start, and provides easy and healthy work together with good wages. The secretary of the industry rides round the district on her bicycle, distributing and collecting the work and giving advice and instruction to the workers.

There are several other isolated examples of outwork, found in different parts of England, which give some idea of the variety of the industries which may adopt the outwork system. There is the weaving of raffia cases for scent bottles and the embroidery of scent sachets which is done for a small factory in Dorset, where lavender water, pot pourri, and eau de cologne are made. Outwork is done for the hatters' furriers at Brandon, Suffolk, about fifty workers being employed by each of the two factories. The processes done at home are called ' opening ' and ' pulling '. The former consists of splitting open the bellies of those skins which come closed and the latter of pulling out the hairs left by the machines on the corners of the skins and the paws. Outworkers are paid ' per turn ', which is a parcel of skins containing five dozen. All except the smallest skins are split by men, but all the pulling is done by women. A species of outwork that fits into agricultural conditions is connected with the pea-picking factories in Boston (Lincs.). When the trade is brisk, usually from September to June, many outworkers are employed; in one factory, in which the maximum number of women indoor hands is four hundred, some hundreds of outworkers also are taken on at the busiest times. The whole family works at the ' picking '— the sorting of the peas and picking out the bad ones. Employment is irregular, a good, dry season involving less pea-picking, as there are fewer bad peas. The work is in no way skilled, although rapidity depends on practice. This work is usually done by the same women who go out on the farms potato-picking from June to September, and therefore fits in well with the agricultural organization of the neighbourhood. In the winter of 1921–2, when there was much unemployment, many families depended for their livelihood on the women's wages from pea-picking.

A mat-making factory in Yorkshire employs a few outworkers on one process, the splicing of the ends of the skeins of coco-nut fibre yarn. A certain amount of knitting in the home for factories used to be done in this county within recent times, although when the district was visited in 1922 no work seemed to have been given out for several years. Stocking-knitting for large hosiery firms was done in the villages of Ravenstonedale and Dent. The orders were all for rather peculiar garments ; stockings thirty-four inches long and thirteen inches in the foot were ordered by the London County Council for sewer men, and somewhat similar ones were required by submarine men, for whom they were ordered by the Admiralty. There may be more of this sort of outwork still done elsewhere, but it is very difficult to trace. In Leicestershire a considerable quantity of hand-knitting is said to be done as outwork for shops. It is unknown to the organized part of the hosiery trade and was more common before the war than to-day. Ringwood, in the New Forest, is noted for its knitted gloves, called ' ringwoods ', which used to be worn by the police, and many outworkers are employed to knit them.

Gloving is probably the industry in which there is the greatest and most widespread amount of outwork. In the south-western counties there are three districts where the work is extensively carried on in the cottages. There are a dozen glove factories in Yeovil and others in the surrounding district. In connexion with these there are depots for the collection and distribution of outwork in the villages for twenty miles around Yeovil. The number of outworkers was given as four thousand in 1921, but it differs from week to week. Torrington is another big centre, with Bideford and Barnstaple as outposts ; silk gloves are the chief manufacture here. The third centre is Westbury (Wilts.), and the work extends from here to Holt and Warminster. Both Yeovil and Westbury make leather gloves, the former producing those of the best quality in all varieties, the latter specializing in hand-sewn gloves of a heavier type.

Worcestershire is another centre of the gloving industry, and here also a large part of the manufacture is done by the outworkers, even in Worcester itself. One of the largest firms has depots, from which the cottage workers are served, at Crowle (near Worcester), Inkborough, Ledbury, and Evesham, and even in Dorset, at Sturminster Newton, and in Devon at Torrington. Another large firm runs a car from its head-quarters in Worcester to serve outworkers in Evesham and the surrounding districts, and in Crowle, Earls Common, Sale Green, Himbleton near Droitwich, and Stock Green near Redditch. This firm also has outworkers in Dorset and a branch factory at Charlbury in Oxfordshire. The latter county is, of course, another great centre of the gloving industry, with many outworkers in the villages. The organization here has been fully described elsewhere.[1]

At Sawston, in Cambridgeshire, there are half a dozen leather-dressing factories, in two or three of which chamois leather gloves are made. At one time many gloves were hand-sewn by cottage workers in this and neighbouring villages, but most of the work is now done by machines in the factories;

[1] K. S. Woods, *The Rural Industries round Oxford*, Oxford University Press, 1921.

as at Westbury, only the rough kinds are now given to out-workers for hand-sewing. At Haverhill, in Suffolk, is another factory from which gloves of the rougher kinds—housemaids', gardening, farm labourers', hedging, and chauffeurs' gloves—are given out to be made up in cottages. Outwork from a factory near Hertford, which makes gloves of the finer sort, is chiefly sent to Devon and Somerset, but there are a few workers in Hertford itself and others in villages within a radius of about six miles.

Another kind of outwork on gloves is found on the borders of Hertfordshire and Bedfordshire, where, in Pirton and Meppershall, there are two small factories with from twenty to forty girls working in each, knitting gloves on hand-worked machines. These provide outwork on ' topping ', or finishing the tips of the fingers.

Processes and Wages.

The processes performed by outworkers in the different industries are many and various, some of them demanding considerable skill, although the tools or apparatus required are usually of a simple nature. Where more elaborate apparatus is used it is often loaned by the firm to the out-worker, and in such cases, of course, the firm is less likely to take on outworkers whom it is not able to keep fairly regularly employed. The gloving industry is peculiarly adapted to the outwork system for several reasons : gloves are light and very easy to transport ; the only tool used is a three-cornered needle, which cuts the leather as it goes through, instead of dragging it as a round one would, and although the work must be carefully done it is not difficult for any woman who is at all skilled with her needle. The gloves given out to be sewn are usually of the coarser kind, on which the work is too heavy to be done by the machines. In the Yeovil district, however, where the gloves made are of the finest quality, the outworkers use treadle-machines. It is usually considered that gloves can be better sewn on the treadle machines than on the power-driven machines used in the factory, although some employers claim that, with skilled workers, the work can be done just as well by power, and of course at a far greater speed.

The ' topping ' of knitted gloves is another very simple process. The method employed is to unravel a few rows at the top of the finger, thread the end of wool and darn through the loops left by the knitting, drawing them together and

finishing them off with two or three stitches. The ' toeing '
and 'seaming ' of the hosiery trade is a similar process.

Other outwork done on treadle-machines is the stitching
of straw hats in the Luton district. The workers are supplied
with ready-made straw plait. The hats which they are
employed to make are chiefly the plain round shapes ; the
fancy shapes, which change from year to year, require more
skill and are usually made in the factory. Power-driven
machines are used in the factories, and the work on the
treadle-machines done by the outworkers is of course more
arduous and slower. The machines are loaned to the workers
from the factory. A certain amount of finishing on hats is
also done by hand.

Another simple process, although of quite a different type,
is that performed by outworkers for a Yorkshire mat factory.
The work is rough and unskilled, and it would seem that a
great part of it could be done equally well by machinery. It
is not, like most outwork, of the kind which can be taken up
and worked on at odd moments. The yarn for the coco-nut
fibre mats comes in bales, each made up of many skeins.
These are given to the outworkers to be spliced. An apparatus known as a ' swift ' is used, consisting of a revolving
frame, on to which a skein of yarn is fixed. The woman
pulls the thread through her hands, the swift revolving with
the skein, and the yarn is unwound on to the ground, forming
what is known as the ' pad '. When a skein runs out she takes
a fresh one, splicing the two ends. She knows by the height
of the heap of yarn when a pad of the right size is complete.
It will be noticed that the woman has to run all the yarn in
each skein through her hands in order only to splice the
ends and to cut off any waste pieces, rough and uneven, at
the ends of the skeins. The yarn is harsh and rough, and
after a day at this uninteresting and poorly paid work
the woman's hands may be swollen and bleeding. One of the
women had formerly worked in a mat-making factory in
London where the skeins were unwound by machinery on to
bobbins.

The process done as home work in the tooth-brush
industry is a skilled one—that of ' drawing ', or putting the
bristles in by hand. Bone brushes cannot be bristled by
machine because the material, being rigid, does not give when
the bristles are pushed into place and the pressure causes the
bone to crack. The handle of the brush is held firm in a vice.
The worker takes from the palm of her hand a bundle of
bristles enough to fill one hole, a loop of wire is pushed from

the back of the brush through the hole bored in the bone, the bristles are passed halfway through the loop and drawn into the hole, doubled and pulled tight. The wire passes then along a groove to the next hole, these grooves being filled in with red or blue cement at the factory, so that the wire is hidden. It requires much practice to gauge the right amount of bristles to fill the hole, and, at the same time, to work quickly ; the workers consider that drawing should be learnt in childhood, from eight years of age upwards. In order to keep pace, steady practice is necessary. A woman who could fill six brushes in an hour when in practice, could only fill four when out of practice.

Straw-plaiting is in many ways one of the most interesting of outwork processes, possessing all the complicated detail of an ancient craft. The plait chiefly made at the present day, however, is one of the simpler kinds, involving a less elaborate preparation of the straw than some of the varieties which used to be made. The straw used for plaiting is bought by the dealer from farmers before it has been through the threshing-machine, and is cut into lengths in the Luton factory, the knots, which spoil the effect of the plait, being cut out. The straw, to be suitable for the purpose, must have a certain length of ' pipe ' between the knots and must be of a clear golden colour and not too brittle. The cut pieces of straw, about twelve inches in length, are sorted into three sizes, and some are dyed. They are then given out to the plaiters. When the straw has to be split the worker uses a small tool, which in Essex has the imposing name of ' engine ', but in Hertfordshire is called simply the splitting-machine or splitter. In the latter county it is a little brass implement, the end hammered into a spike bent at right angles, with five, six, seven, or eight tiny blades set round it, to split the straw into the number of pieces required. This spike is put into the straw and the blades are pressed gently down until the straw splits. The split straws are pressed in a ' roller mill ', a kind of miniature mangle turned by a handle and secured to a plank or to a beam of the house. The straw is now ready to plait. Many different patterns can be made, some more difficult than others. The simplest is done with seven straws, but even this is extremely difficult for the beginner. The straws, being small and slippery, are not easily put into position, and even when in place they are apt, being very springy, to jump back again. Care must be taken not to break them. With some of the more elaborate plaits there is a difficulty in understanding and remembering how to make

the pattern. 'Thirteen diamond' is one of the most difficult to do and 'English brilliant' is one of the most famous
of the old plaits, but not so difficult as many to carry out.
Certain villages in Hertfordshire seem to have specialized
in particular patterns, which may help to account for the
survival of the industry chiefly in Offley, which happened
to produce the pattern most used at the present day. This
is the 'rustic', which is made, not with split, but with whole
straws. It is started with two straws, each bent in the
middle, fresh ones being worked in as each gives out. 'Notch'
is another pattern made with whole straws. 'Rough side'
was made with seven pieces of split straw with the yellow side
up. 'Smooth side' was a similar plait, but with the shining
white inner side of the split straw uppermost. 'Twist' was
another pattern made with split straws.

After an ordinary straw plait is made it must be 'speeled',
i. e. the projecting ends of straw cut off, for, as a fresh piece
of straw is worked in, the shortest piece is left sticking out.
Most of the plait now made in Hertfordshire is done with
whole straws, but in Meppershall, in 1923, some plait had
been made of split straws for the first time for many years.
Splitters had been lent by the dealers, but rolling mills were
not supplied, so if the workers did not possess these they had
to work with the rough straw, the sharp edges of which were
apt to cut their hands. Some, however, put the straws
through an ordinary mangle.

Ordinarily, straw-plaiting is carried on from soon after the
harvest, when straw becomes available, until May or June.
The busiest time is in the spring, but some of the plaiting
villages, when visited in May 1923, had only had a few weeks'
work during the previous twelve months.

The outwork done in connexion with the doll industry of
Braxted, near Witham in Essex, is of a simple kind. The
skilled part of the work, the making of the moulds in which
the composition heads are cast, is done by a skilled worker.
The outworkers merely press the composition into the
moulds, getting it smooth and even and removing it at the
right moment. Others paint and polish the faces, and others
again make the arms, legs, and bodies, sewing up the shapes
and stuffing them. Others make the dolls' clothing. No
worker does more than one process. Sometimes, if she is
manifestly unsuccessful with one, she may be given a chance
of trying another.

Outworkers are to be found in the greatest numbers in the

south-western counties and in Worcestershire. There are sometimes as many as four thousand employed around Yeovil on glove-making, but in North Devon the number is not a quarter of this and in the Westbury district it is still smaller. Around Sawston (Cambs.) the outwork (hand-sewing of the rougher kinds of gloves) is chiefly done by the wives of men employed in the factory, and not more than a dozen women, each having a few dozen pairs of gloves weekly to sew, are employed. In Hertfordshire the number of local women who sew gloves in their homes varied between 1920 and 1923 from thirty-eight to twenty, though here, as in other places where outwork is done, there is a great fluctuation in the numbers employed from week to week. Around Haverhill (Suffolk) there are about a hundred and twenty workers within a radius of four miles.

The amount earned varies according to skill and speed and also according to district and process. Gloving work of a high standard, such as that done near Worcester, takes a year or so to learn, and the rates are higher than for the poorer sort, but as the work cannot be done very rapidly the women often do not earn more. In 1923 the Haverhill workers could earn £1 a week for sewing rough gloves, if they worked full time, which outworkers never do. In Hertfordshire the best workers were earning from 15s. to 25s a week in 1923, the latter being the maximum paid to any outworker. Others earned much less. When new outworkers are taken on here they often work in the factory for a week or two until proficient.

The earnings of workers on treadle machines in the Yeovil district in 1923 were from about £1 a week to 25s., £1 being the unit on which the employer pays the health insurance contribution, and therefore the estimated average rate of full time earnings. Handwork earnings here are at the rate of about half per hour of what can be earned on a machine. Very few handworkers earned as much as £1 a week, and if they did it 'took them all their time'. The greater number were earning perhaps 5s. weekly by doing a few pairs in their spare time. They could pick up the work at odd moments, and found the hand-sewing pleasanter and lighter than sitting at a machine. There are few who are entirely dependent on glove-sewing for a livelihood. The work is chiefly done by the married women, though some of the girls in Somerset who work on the machines are more dependent upon it. The machines usually belong to the employer, but occasionally the worker has her own and works for any firm.

Against these workers the accusation was brought that when work was plentiful and wages rose the output of each individual declined and many new workers had to be taught. The old workers were used to taking about £1 a week and would not trouble to earn more. The hours necessary to bring in this sum did not represent a full week's work according to factory hours.

There were in 1922 from twenty to thirty outworkers topping gloves in and around Pirton (Herts.) and Meppershall (Beds.). Many of them were the mothers of girls working in the factories and others were girls who were waiting for a place inside. A few were former employees who had left to be married. This work is unskilled. It takes less than a minute to 'top' each finger. The payment was 3½d. for twenty-four 'hands', which takes about two hours, or possibly less, to do. The women could not estimate the time occupied as, like most home workers, they pick up the work at odd moments. Each receives only a few dozen pairs each week to do, so the earnings are small.

In Hertfordshire the wives of farm labourers used to plait straw to supplement the family income, and the men also did it occasionally in winter on days when there was no farm work. Plaiting was, like lace-making, taught in special schools, where boys and girls spent an hour or two in learning to read and write and do sums, and the rest of the day in plaiting. Other children learnt at home, generally at the age of five or six. The hours were from nine to twelve and from two to five, and each child had to finish a certain number of yards per day before it left the school. The parents paid 2d. a week, but other cases were mentioned in which the children were paid a small sum for their work. Possibly this arrangement depended upon their proficiency. The points that chiefly stood out in the memory of one old woman who described a plait school were the half-yard rule with which the work was measured before the children were allowed to go, and the break occasioned by Bible readings at eleven o'clock every morning. The children had rhymes to help them to remember how the straws had to be plaited, such as :

'Over one and under two,
Pull it tight and that will do.'

The payment for straw-plaiting was not quite so low as that for lace-making.[1] Threepence a yard was paid for 'Thirteen diamond', and in an hour one and a half yards of

---

[1] Cf. Vol. III, *Decorative Crafts.* Lace Making.

this pattern could be made by a very good worker. Of the simple seven-straw plait a good worker could make six yards an hour. In 1923 the Luton dealer stated that a hundred and fifty yards a week was the average amount of straw plait received from each woman. One worker had a coil of nine score yards ready for him. The payment for ' rustic ' plait at this time was 3*d*. a score of yards, and about ten yards can be made in an hour. The payment may vary with the quality of the work, and the speed of the worker depends on the straw, which is at its best for plaiting soon after the harvest. In May, at the end of the busy season, most of the women seemed to be doing from twelve to eighteen hours' plaiting weekly and earning from 2*s*. to 4*s*. When a considerable quantity of an easy pattern known as the ' widdle-waddle ' [1] was wanted in a hurry, the workers were paid at the rate of 9*d*. for a score of yards, which could be plaited in an hour. This high rate was evidently paid in order to persuade as many people as possible to undertake it, for normally the amount earned per hour would be less than a fourth of this. The workers pay for the straw received, but this payment is refunded to them when the plait is collected, and the earnings mentioned are the actual amount paid for work, exclusive of this amount payable on the material. The fact that one hundred and fifty yards of Chinese plait could at this time be bought for 7½*d*. shows clearly the reason for the decline of the English straw-plaiting industry.

In a small straw hat workshop in Markyate, near Luton, the girls employed indoors were earning, on an average, from 25*s*. to 35*s*. weekly in 1923, and some of the outdoor workers seemed able to earn the same amount, in spite of their disadvantage of having to work on treadle machines. Perhaps this is because they were more experienced workers than the girls employed in the factory ; they did not appear to be working for excessively long hours. One employer said that his best outworker could earn 10*s*. by a steady day's work, and it could be seen from the wages book that she often earned £2 10*s*. in a week. Some of the factories make straw hats for export to South Africa and elsewhere, and in this case the amount of work done remains the same throughout the year. Most of the outworkers, however, are only employed from September to Whitsun, although many factories keep the same number of indoor hands engaged throughout the year by making felt hats during the summer. This

[1] This work is the braiding of long, ready-made plaits of grass, not straw-plaiting in the ordinary sense.

irregularity in the work is doubtless the reason for the employment of outworkers in this industry. Many of the village workers, both at home and in the factories, were, when the district was visited in 1923, earning more than their husbands where the latter were farm hands or gardeners.

In the doll industry at Braxted during the war the outworkers included wounded men and those on leave. The workers now are chiefly women and girls, of all classes, but there are also a few men and boys who are unable to find other work. This is one of the best paid varieties of outwork, and doubtless this is partly due to the fact that the organizers of the industry are not dependent on it for a living, but only need to cover expenses, since they carry on the enterprise as a philanthropic one. Thus it is not really self-supporting. Up to 1923 the wages had not been reduced since the war. For the first process on the doll's head—simply pressing the composition into the mould—which takes half an hour, 4d. was paid. 1s. was paid for making a dress set for a doll. The workers were earning from 30s. to 50s. a week according to the amount of time they put in. One girl boasted that she could earn 30s. a week and yet play tennis every afternoon. At the busiest time there were fifty workers in the immediate neighbourhood of Witham, twenty at Hatfield Peveril, another twenty at Kelvedon, and others in other villages. There were also branches in Yorkshire and Kent. By 1923 the number of workers had been greatly reduced. The season for doll-making is the autumn. The orders come in August and September and the work starts in October and November and has to be done by Christmas. The slackest season is January and February, which is also the slackest season on a farm, so that the industry does not supplement farm work very conveniently, although it is chiefly done by the wives of agricultural labourers. The organizers of the business have a certain amount of work to do in January, and every other year they give out a little to be done by the outworkers in preparation for a trade exhibition in February.

The ribbon-weaving outworkers of the Coventry district are all elderly women. This sort of weaving has been women's work for a long time, if not from the beginning of the craft, although the heavier work of weaving materials was normally done by men. Not more than half a dozen new ribbon-weavers have started work within the last twenty years and there is no demand for new looms. The earnings on ribbon-weaving are very small. The maximum which could be earned in

K 2

1923 was £1 a week, and that was for hours much longer than those worked in a factory. It must also be borne in mind that this work is not of the type which can be picked up and done at odd moments. The loom, which is a big, cumbersome apparatus, is the property of the worker; she usually works steadily at it for considerable periods of time at a stretch and the work is fairly arduous. The male velvet-weavers in Sudbury were slightly better paid, 29s. a week being their maximum earnings.

Hand-frame knitting is skilled work and it takes an apprentice two years to learn it thoroughly. After that, when working forty-eight hours a week, he could, in 1921, only earn £2. Those engaged in making elastic bandages rose to as high as £3 a week. The wages for this occupation are higher than those of most outworkers because it is done as a full-time job. The worker has his own ' shop ', in which he works regular hours, and he relies on what he earns for his complete livelihood.

The earnings on outwork connected with the lace and hosiery industries are very low. The National Health Insurance unit, which is based on what an average worker in the trade is supposed to be able to do in a forty-eight hour week, was, in 1920–1, 16s. for lace-workers, 10s. for chever-ning, and 11s. 6d. for linking and seaming hosiery by machine. Net-mending is fine work and cannot easily be picked up by adults, but girls fresh from school take to it ' like ducks to water '. Beginners, of course, take much longer than a week to achieve their 16s. unit. Hand-knitting in Leicestershire seemed to be even more poorly paid, the workers saying that they had to work late at night in order to earn 1s. a day.

There were only two persons engaged on the outwork for the Yorkshire mat factory when this was visited in 1922. Both were married women. Each received one hundred-weight of yarn three times a week; one hundredweight represents half a day's work, and the pay for splicing this amount was 1s. 9d.

Rates of remuneration are impossible to calculate for the shuttlecock-makers. All members of the family work from their earliest years and have every chance of acquiring the necessary speed and skill. The conditions in which the family lived pointed to low earnings for all concerned. The cocks were sold to shops in Nottingham for 1½d. each. Out of this sum the maker had to provide all materials, which include white feathers, wood and cork, strapping, velvet, and glue. The retail price was 3d. each. All the members of the

shuttlecock-making family seemed to be intelligent and highly
skilled workers, but their hours were long, their earnings low,
and the work was carried on under the poorest conditions, in
a badly lighted, badly ventilated room in a poor court. In
a factory they would probably have worked under far more
comfortable conditions and have earned more. The fact that
they were independent of factory hours and regulations
seems to be the only advantage which their trade gave them,
apart from the fact that it was invested with something of
the glamour of an ancient craft. The maker, in spite of the
sordid conditions in which he worked, seemed to be conscious
of this, and boasted that there was no other maker of shuttle-
cocks nearer than Leeds. The industry, curiously enough, is
a seasonal one. From Christmas to Shrove Tuesday is the
busy time for the makers. Shrove Tuesday is the opening
day of the ' shuttlecock season '. The investigator, hap-
pening to cycle through some twenty villages on that day,
noticed that nearly every child was playing with a shuttlecock.

Outwork on tooth-brushes is done more by girls than by
married women. They are able to give a good deal of time
to it, and in 1921 they could earn in the week the 30s. unit
on which the employer was liable for his National Health
Insurance contribution. The Trade Board rate was 9d. an
hour. For bristling a half gross box, 8s. 9d. to 9s. was paid,
according to the kind of brush. The work is clean and convenient, but monotonous.

Organization and Conditions.

The organization of outwork differs in detail in the different
industries, but the main outlines of the system are much the
same everywhere. The outworkers call for their work at the
factory or at a depot, or it is taken to their homes in vans.
Finished articles are collected and paid for and new work is
distributed at the same time. The payment is always by piece
rates and the work is done in the worker's own time. Work
is, as a general rule, returned weekly, although in some
industries no question is raised if it is kept longer. In most
cases, however, even when the work is not collected by a van,
the worker's need of the wages probably causes her to return
it regularly.

The most highly organized outwork system was found in
the gloving industry around Worcester, where there are
village depots for the collection of the work. There are also
depots within a radius of about twenty miles around Yeovil.

From Worcester a motor van takes a ' server ' and a clerk once a week to some cottage where a room is hired and where they receive made-up gloves and give out wages and more work. The server is herself a skilled worker, and where the relations between employer and outworkers are friendly these meetings take on a social character.

In the hand-knitting industry for shops the woman who receives the wool from the shop may, in her turn, give it out to other workers on her own responsibility.

All the Warwickshire ribbon-weavers now work for a big Coventry firm. The only survivor of several smaller firms is a middleman, who receives the material from a Coventry firm, gives it out to local weavers, collects the woven ribbons from them and returns them to the factory. Since the wages earned even by those weavers who work direct for the factory are very small, it is difficult to imagine how the industry stands the addition of the middleman.

Unlike most forms of outwork hand-frame knitting is a regular trade with hours and wages of its own, and a workshop where it is carried on is treated as a factory in itself. The custom is for a firm to set up eight or ten machines for a man in a workshop, to supply him regularly with wool or silk and the orders for garments, and to pay him piece rates for all articles finished and brought in. It is left to him to engage and pay the other workers in his shop.

Gloving, net-mending, and many finishing processes are obviously suited to outwork, from the manufacturer's point of view. The materials are easily transported and the processes are easily learnt and more cheaply or better done by hand than by machine. There are certain industries which are less easily adaptable to the conditions of homework in which, nevertheless, the system has been adopted extensively. Such, for example, is the brush industry of the south-western counties, in which the bristling is done by outworkers, although it is a process requiring considerable skill. In an industry of this kind more careful organization of the outwork system is necessary, to train the workers, to sift the good work from the bad, and to keep in touch with those who do the best. The secretary of the Braxted doll industry makes frequent visits to all the workers to examine the quality of the work and to study the individual capacity of the employees in relation to processes, adapting the work given out to each according to what she finds. In the case of an ordinary business firm the time spent by a highly qualified employee in this manner would subtract from the saving on overhead charges which is one of the most important aspects of outwork from the employer's point of view.

Where machines are provided by the factory the problem becomes still more complicated. Outwork on some machine or apparatus may be regarded as a survival of an old system. The weaving industry developed from the stage when it was carried on by independent craftsmen, or in small workshops, to the next stage, in which it was an outwork industry, each man working his own loom in his own cottage, but receiving orders and raw materials from a wholesale firm. In the Coventry ribbon-weaving we see a relic of this system. In the rather more modern hand-frame knitting industry we find the same system, the frames being the property of the workers. Here, as amongst the Coventry weavers, all the workers are elderly and no new machines are being set up. Possibly these employees were originally independent workers. In other cases, however, as, for example, the straw hat industry in the Luton district and a branch of the gloving industry around Yeovil, machines are supplied by the firm. Here it is more difficult to understand why the outwork system is adopted. Unless the outworkers can be kept fairly regularly employed, the capital expended on the machines is wasting, and when an employee moves from the district or gives up the work for other reasons, the firm has to dispose of the machine. One of the great attractions of outwork for the woman with a house to look after—that it takes up no room and can be picked up at odd moments— is lacking when machines must be used.

Outwork in relation to social and economic conditions in rural districts has its good and bad aspects. The system is often condemned as helping to keep down agricultural wages below a reasonable level by providing a possibility of supplementary earnings for the labourer's family. Moreover, the fact that outworkers are seldom entirely dependent upon their earnings renders the system peculiarly liable to the evils of sweating. The earnings of the Oxfordshire gloveresses before the war were notoriously low. The poor conditions of agricultural labourers in Oxon and Dorset have been attributed in part to the outwork systems in force in these counties. Then too, homes can be as badly neglected through outwork, especially when it is done under the urgent necessity of earning a supplementary wage, as they may be where the housewife goes out to work, and the additional evil of child labour has to be considered. When several members of a family all work together in a small, close cottage room, the home is converted into a factory of the worst type. In Hertfordshire, where agricultural wages are higher than in most counties where outwork abounds, a gloving factory is unable to find sufficient local outworkers, in spite of a possible maximum of 25s. a week to be earned in this way, and gloves are sent from here to be sewn in Somerset and Devon.

The system has its obvious disadvantages from the employer's point of view. He often finds outworkers unsatisfactory because he cannot rely on them to finish their work within a certain time. It was said that the knitters of Ringwood gloves not only failed sometimes to execute orders, but did not even return the wool. In any industry the materials given out to home workers must be carefully weighed or measured and checked on return. Another disadvantage is that there is no one to oversee the workers and prevent bad work. It is one of the duties of the ' servers ', or whoever gives out and returns work, to criticize its quality and advise the workers, but a great quantity may be badly done before there is any chance of correcting it.

Outwork is subject to more violent fluctuations than any other form of employment. The workers having in nearly all cases taken it up because they are tied to their homes, cannot, if they are dismissed, find other employment or move to another district, and they are therefore ready for the employer when they are next needed. While they stand idle he incurs no expense in the shape of overhead charges for factory accommodation, and they, being partially supported from other sources, are able to exist even when their source of earnings runs dry. The outwork system is therefore often used as a means of getting an elastic labour supply during booms in the trade, and many people condemn it on the grounds that employers use it to avoid the expense of factory organization and regulations by having this labour supply to utilize in times of pressure. Since outworkers are scattered, and their conditions of work so irregular, any organization among them is almost impossible.

In the gloving industry of Worcestershire and Herefordshire the other side of the picture is seen. The Worcester firm finds its most satisfactory workers in the Evesham market-gardening and fruit-farming district, where agricultural conditions are on a high level. The women who work in the gardens or orchards during the summer find gloving a convenient winter occupation. This firm will open a depot in any village where they are assured of thirty workers, of whom a number must be young girls. A tour in the glove van, which stops at the road side in hamlets where there are too few workers for a room to be engaged, opens the eyes to the social possibilities of the system, particularly where there is the right type of woman to supervise the work and deal with the women tactfully and patiently.

In some kinds of outwork there are obviously advantages to the outworkers themselves. To independent temperaments it is more satisfactory to choose the hours of work, even if these are longer in the end than those in a factory. Again, it suits married women who may have many odd moments to give to it, but who could not leave home for the day. Delicate girls, also, often find it a convenient occupation. In the Bridgwater district girls who are not strong enough for willow-peeling (in connexion with the osier and basket industries) often do gloving at home. Some types of outwork, such as knitting, provide a good occupation for elderly women whose sight may be failing. Though the sewing of the silk gloves made at Torrington does not combine well with house work, since smooth hands are needed, the hand-sewing of leather gloves is particularly suitable for home workers. The Coventry ribbon-weavers, although they complain of the low rate of wages, have a good deal to say in favour of the outwork system. They find their work enjoyable and not so wearisome as it looks to an observer. Nevertheless they own that they would be sorry to think that any of their daughters should depend on ribbon-weaving for a livelihood. A Lancashire woman who had gone to live in a Lincolnshire village expressed the opinion that clothing factories, such as she had worked for in her own county, which would give out button-holing or finishing work to be done at home, would be an asset to the district. She herself was in comfortable circumstances, and she had considered the question intelligently and not from a merely personal point of view. From her own experience and observation she considered outwork as beneficial to village women.

Outworkers who do the more highly skilled types of work are in a more satisfactory position than others, because their employer cannot get new workers at a moment's notice and is therefore reluctant to lose touch with those who are already expert. Some firms which cease to serve outworkers for several months in slack times of trade, give precedence, when there is not enough work for all, to the unmarried women, as it is considered more disastrous for them to be suddenly deprived of their livelihood.

Certain types of outwork are decidedly on the decrease. At one time a great deal of hand-finishing of machine-made garments was done by cottage women in the Midlands, but as machinery is improved it ceases to be necessary for the manufacturer to send his goods out to be finished under conditions which he cannot supervise. The only one of such processes which seems to have a future as outwork is the lace-mending of the Nottingham and Honiton districts. A net-mending room opened in the latter town in 1921 was popular, and in Nottingham it was said that the lack of outwork in that year was due only to the trade slump and not to any permanent change in the organization of the industry.

The stocking-knitting of Yorkshire has now stopped because the knitters earned only 3s. or 4s. a week and younger women will not take on the work at that price. Similarly the Coggeshall bead-work, which is done for an East End firm for a few months of the year, is not likely to last long since the pay is very low. Straw-plaiting is another form of outwork which seems likely to die out before very long, owing, in this case, to foreign competition in the same industry. Japanese and Chinese plait are both lighter and cheaper than the English variety, as well as whiter in colour. English straw is tougher and more durable, and makers of hats who have used both kinds say that English plait is easier to work up. Wearers of hats, however, value lightness and cheapness more than durability, and except for a few special purposes there is no longer any great demand for English plait.

In the Sudbury silk factory it was stated that the weaving of umbrella silk would be done by power as soon as capital was available to install it. The two old hand-weavers still at work here are the survivors of about four hundred. Another firm, at Haverhill, still employs nine old workers to weave umbrella silk, but doubtless this form of outwork will cease with the lives of the workers, if not before. It is still impossible to weave by power certain rich silks, such as that used for some kinds of ties, for furniture and coat linings and for the revers of men's dinner jackets, but even where hand-work is retained, as at Braintree and Sudbury, it is now done inside the factory, and not as outwork. The only kinds of ribbon now given out to the Coventry firms to be woven by hand are hat bands in school and club colours, of which only a few dozen yards are required, for which it is not worth while to set up a power loom. The latter makes from eighteen to thirty pieces at once, and needs only one person to tend the machinery. There are still enough workers to make all the ribbons needed, though it seems possible that the time may come when the firm will be forced either to make up these short lengths by machinery or else to increase the rates of pay in order to persuade a few new workers to learn. Young women prefer factory work, and would probably still do so even if they could earn better wages at home than they now can. Thirty or forty years ago the girls in villages where the ribbon-weaving industry flourished would learn weaving from their mothers at fourteen or fifteen years of age, as soon as they were old enough to work the loom. At present there are hardly any weavers under fifty, though probably a fair number of younger women learnt the craft in their youth, but have ceased to practise it. No girls learn now, and the number of workers seems bound to dwindle. Owing to the expensive and cumbersome appliances that are needed, this industry is not likely to be kept alive, as lace-making is, by women who are glad in old age to practise in spare moments a craft which will bring them in a few extra shillings weekly.

The hand-frame knitting, which is done in cottage workshops, is being rapidly superseded by power machines in factories. A man can work eight machines by power where he can only work one by hand. In one of the villages near Nottingham, where there is a workshop with nine machines in it, there are never more than four in use at the best of times, and the men are all old. This state of affairs is largely due to the low wages. The only branch of frame-knitting by hand which has a future is that for making up elastic silk stockings and knee-caps and other woven silk goods for surgical use. Nearly all of these are made to measure and therefore the hand machine is cheaper, since to set up a power machine to make one, or even half a dozen, articles involves waste of time and money. In one workshop with twelve machines making surgical bandages, every one of them was working full time, even in the winter of 1921. The Belper outwork industry in fine silk underwear was then at a standstill.

The possibility of sweated outwork in some industries should be closely watched. The helplessness of outworkers in the hands of unscrupulous employers, who might use the possibilities of the system in their own interests exclusive of those of their employees, is a danger to the community, which is injured in the suffering of any of its members. On the other hand, to attempt to avoid this evil by sweeping away the whole system would be to lose the benefits which can be seen in those districts where it is working at its best. The social possibilities of outwork ought not to be neglected. Because it involves so many different industries as well as districts, and the conditions vary so widely, the question of the desirability of outwork is not one which can be judged as a whole, but each part must be studied in relation to local conditions.

The whole question of outwork has many points in common with that of the home crafts and industries.[1] Some of the handicraft enterprises are organized on an outwork system, somewhat akin to that of the Braxted doll industry. It seems that the greatest possibility for the future development of outwork lies in this direction. The difficulty of ensuring uniformity of work becomes of less importance the more an industry is developed on the lines of artistic craftwork, whilst at the same time individuality and the capacity for original design, which are more likely to be found in home workers than in factory hands, become of greater value.

The arts and crafts movement, which has made great headway in recent years, aims at reviving and developing along new lines the best features of ancient craftwork, and it is possible that the outworkers, the modern representatives of the old village craftsmen, will come to take an important place in the scheme.

---

[1] See Vol. III, *Decorative Crafts*.

SOME SMALL RURAL FACTORIES

A VERY large number of the small factories and work-shops which are described in this chapter owed their foundation to some local supply of raw material, although many of them have now ceased to depend upon these local resources.

Brush-making, i. e. bristling and finishing, is carried on by many small firms in Somerset, Dorset, and Devon, which obtain the turned stocks, or backs, from the small turneries using locally-grown wood. The brushes made by these firms are marketed locally.

Tanneries and boot factories at one time flourished in close connexion throughout the south-western counties, but the rural branches of these industries have declined considerably. Tanneries are now very few and far between, and many of the small workshops and factories which, until lately, manufactured boots, have been closed. A factory in one of the towns on the Dartmoor borders which specializes in heavy farm boots for sale in local towns and villages is still carried on successfully. The connexion between local boot factories and tanneries is now very slight. Some country tanneries still survive which retain the character of rural industries ; [1] others, on factory lines, are to be found in the larger towns.

The Wilton carpet industry,[2] which is more fully described elsewhere, because it is chiefly of interest as an example of hand-loom weaving, is a survival of the once famous woollen industries connected with the great flocks of sheep which grazed on the Wiltshire Downs and Salisbury Plain, although it no longer has any connexion with locally-grown wool. There is one central factory, and four branches in neighbouring villages.

Blanket-weaving in Cumberland and Westmorland is another industry which owes its origin to the local prevalence of sheep-farming, and one which still has some direct connexion with it. There are several blanket and cloth mills of moderate size in these counties, and it was until recently

---

[1] See *Timber and Underwood Industries and Some Village Workshops*, Chap. III, Oak-bark Tanning.
[2] Cf. Vol. III, *Decorative Crafts*, Chap. III.

the custom for each farmer to send the fleeces of his own flock to the mill, where this wool was separately carded, spun and woven, and returned to him in the form of cloth or blankets. A certain amount of wool is still supplied to these mills by local farmers, but all that comes in is now thrown together and sorted, and the farmer chooses from amongst the stock which comes to his door in the firm's motor van a selection of goods equivalent to the value of his wool.

Perfume distilleries, depending upon locally-grown lavender, are sometimes situated in country towns. One in Dorset makes use of lavender grown in cottage gardens of the district, and for the potpourri also made here, of bog myrtle blossoms collected by children from the New Forest. The whole product of this factory is sold abroad. Quantities of lavender are grown round about Hitchin, and there are two distilleries in the town, owned by the growers. In one case this industry is carried on in connexion with a chemist's shop, all kinds of toilet requisites perfumed with lavender being made and sold here. The lavender industry around Hitchin is said to have decreased in recent years, and Mitcham is now the chief centre. In growing lavender the soil and situation are of great importance, and Mitcham seems to be an ideal district from this point of view. Unless the flowers are to be marketed fresh, or dried and sold only for sachet-making, &c., there must be a distillery near at hand, so that the spikes of flowers, having been cut in the sun and spread out to dry during the day, may be carried to the distillery in the evening and placed in the still without delay.

The pea factories of Boston owe their situation to the extensive cultivation of peas on the light lands of Kesteven. Boston has been the centre of the ' pea-industry ' since its origin forty years ago, but there are also factories in Spalding and Bourne, in Lincoln, and in Peterborough. Boston, although still an important market centre for a large agricultural district, has the characteristics and organization of an industrial town, including day-nurseries for the children of working women ; Peterborough and Lincoln are industrial centres of considerable importance, but Spalding and Bourne are more rural. The pea factories, however, have an important connexion with the rural districts, although they draw their labour chiefly from the town population. The intensive cultivation of the rich Fenlands provides work for women in the fields almost all the year round, on potato-lifting, fruit-picking, and other seasonal jobs, the busiest time being from May to October. Although peas which are sold to be eaten in their fresh state are picked by hand, those for the factories are harvested and threshed, and must then be picked over, sorted, and the bad ones taken out before being put into packets for sale. Great numbers of women are employed on this work, both in the factories and as outworkers, and in the slack season of the factories, from June to September, these same women work on the land, being employed under the gang system, and taken out from the towns in motor lorries to their work.

A hatters' furriery is a curious industry established at Brandon (Suffolk), and owing its origin there to the great numbers of rabbits which inhabit the sandy wastes in that district. The industry has, however, developed to such an extent that the skins now come from markets all over England. At Thetford, near by, at Swaffham, and elsewhere in East Anglia, there are dealers who own or rent hundreds of acres of these commons, useless for any kind of cultivation, and make a good living by catching or killing the rabbits, which are sold alive for coursing, or dead for food. Thousands of imported rabbits, mainly from Australia, also contribute their coats to this industry.

Few of the rural factories of any considerable size owe their origin solely or mainly to the existence of a local market for their output, although many of them sell a proportion of their goods in neighbouring towns or villages. There is seldom so extensive a demand for any one article from a single agricultural district as to lead to the establishment of a factory to make the article on the spot ; the extent of the demand is more often such as can be supplied by a small workshop or a number of scattered individual workers. Baskets provide an exception ; they are used in thousands in the chief fruit-growing areas, but great quantities of them are imported, the English method of small workshop production having failed in the competition with the probably better-organized industry abroad.[1] In the case, however, of one of the ' non-returnable ', cheap and flimsy packages which are replacing wicker baskets to a great extent for the packing of certain kinds of fruit, mass factory production in the neighbourhood of the fruit-growing districts is meeting the demand.

Chip baskets for strawberries are now made in factories which are to be found in the Fen country, at Wisbech, in

[1] See Part I, Chap. II. *Osier Growing and Basket Making.*

the south-west of England at Calstock (in the Tamar Valley), Swanwick, and Cheddar, as well as on the outskirts of London and in Glasgow. As a factory industry this is a fairly recent one in England, and it made great headway during the restriction of imports caused by the war ; it seems, unlike the wicker basket industry, to be well able to hold its own against the foreign competition to which it is now once more subject. Most of the factories are on a fairly large scale, as many as a hundred girls being employed in some of them, but at Cheddar the industry was still to be found in 1921 in the form of a survival of an old cottage industry, and here there were only two small workshops. This is the only place in which any trace has been found of chip-basket making as an old rural industry in which the work was done by hand. It formed a winter occupation for farm workers, who split the wood by hand into the thin flat strips which are plaited into baskets. They probably used the locally grown poplar, willow, and fir, which came into use again during the war, when the Russian aspen and Newfoundland spruce, which are now considered the best material, were not available. Machinery is now generally used for slicing up the wood, and the plaiting processes which must be done by hand are subdivided to such an extent that each girl has only to perform one simple action and then hand the basket on to the next worker.

A mixed wood-ware factory in Hampshire, where veneers for brush backs, brush stocks, sieve hoops, and other small articles were made, had also at one time produced chip-baskets for the Swanwick district. In the other places, however, the chip-baskets seem to have been the sole output of the factories, except at Cheddar, where one of the small workshops combined this industry with general sawing work for wheelwrights and builders. Where the industry was carried on in connexion with other work, it was on a small scale, and the machinery used was of a comparatively simple type. The larger factories, representing the latest development of the industry, use highly specialized machinery. Some of them were, when visited, extending rapidly, and it seems likely that the smaller and more old-fashioned firms will soon be swamped by the larger ones.

Of the oddly situated little industries which seem to owe their existence mainly to the presence of an available and otherwise untapped supply of labour—and, in some cases perhaps, an empty building—there are numerous examples in the south-west of England and elsewhere. The following four different examples may be taken as fairly typical.

Machine-knitting, or ' fashioned knitting ', as it is technically called, is quite extensively carried on in Devon and Cornwall. In 1921 there were about sixteen knitting factories and workshops in these counties, employing rather more than eight hundred and fifty workers. This number included one hundred and sixty in a Plymouth factory, and nearly two hundred in two branches of another firm at Newquay and Redruth, but the other thirteen factories or workshops employed from eighty down to only ten workers, nearly all women and girls, and many of them were in thoroughly rural districts. A small workshop of the same type, in which three girls were employed, was found in Hampshire. In one of the workrooms, fashioned knitting had replaced hand-weaving at the beginning of the war. Most of the work is done for the more fashionable shops of London and large towns.

The tooth-brush industry in Devon is represented by two firms with factories at Axminster and in the village of Nummer, four miles from Chard. Several hundreds of out-workers are employed, in fact, they outnumber the indoor hands ; [1] many of them are women and girls working in their homes in the villages within a ten-mile radius of Axminster.

The collar factories which are to be found in many Devon and Somerset towns also employ outworkers to some extent for the simpler processes, but in this case the bulk of the work is done in the factories, chiefly by girls and unmarried women, although married women are also employed.

The glove industry has three chief centres in the south-western counties, at Yeovil on the borders of Somerset and Dorset, at Torrington in North Devon, and at Westbury in Wilts. There are numerous factories in towns and villages in all these districts ; great numbers of outworkers are employed, four thousand being the number estimated of those at work in their homes within twenty miles of Yeovil at a busy season. Torrington is the home of the silk glove industry, although a few leather gloves are also made here. In the Westbury and Yeovil districts leather gloves are made, of a rather heavier variety in the former place. At Yeovil the industry is closely connected with the leather-dressing industry, which, however, is not rural ; at Barnstaple, in the Torrington district, there is also one leather-dressing

[1] See p. 119.

and glove factory, where leather bags and hats are also made, and at Holt, in Wiltshire, there is a leather-dressing factory of a more rural character, local sheepskins being dressed and made up into gloves. The skins are coloured in delicate shades of buff and grey, a process which is said to be very difficult with English skins, since they are, as a rule, too greasy to take the colour. This seems to be the only factory of the kind in England which makes use of fells obtained locally.

The manager of a glove factory in the East Midlands stated that the women of the West Country were more skilled in the sewing of gloves than their countrywomen in any other part of England ; from this particular factory many gloves are sent to Somerset to be sewn by the out-workers there, although it is not fifty miles away from Olney, the centre of the Bedford and Buckingham lace-making district, where, it would be supposed, the village women have fingers more skilled in delicate and exacting work than anywhere else in the country. Within even easier reach of this factory is the district where the straw-plaiting industry, in which the work requires considerable manual dexterity, still survives. Both the lace-making and the straw-plaiting industries seem to be rapidly dying out, because lace can be made more cheaply in factories and straw-plait bought more cheaply abroad. Yet small rural factories, utilizing the labour of these skilled women, either in their homes or in workshops, have not sprung up in these districts to any extent, although one might have thought that here would be an opening for them. In the straw-plaiting district there are a few small workshops where knitted gloves are made on machines operated by hand by girls, the gloves being given to outworkers to be finished. This industry, however, is on a very small scale at present, although possibly it may be further developed. In Olney itself there is a boot factory, one of the outposts of the Northamptonshire industry, and the girls from the neighbouring villages can earn more in the factory in a week than they could in many laborious weeks spent at the lace-pillow. Probably the nearness of this locality to the big industrial centres, and to London itself, accounts for the fact that small rural factories do not seem to flourish here. Any surplus population, both male and female, migrates to the larger towns with their greater opportunities for amusement and education.

Curious little industries occur here and there, of each of which one example only probably exists. Such a one was

chanced upon in Yorkshire, where the inquirer after rural
industries was once told that ' The only rural industry in
Yorkshire is staining Honesty red '. The explanation was
discovered in a village within five miles of Scarborough,
whence, it was said, labour would be easily obtainable when
more was needed for the little industry which was started
here a few years ago. Bushes of honesty are cultivated on
a few acres of land ; when the seeds are ripe the branches
are cut and dried, after which the brown outer husks are
pulled off by hand, revealing the flat, silvery seed-cases.
The branches are then dipped—barbarously, and it would
seem to the ordinary observer, most unnecessarily—into
vats of dye, and emerge in horrible and unnatural tints of
crimson, purple, metallic green, and crude yellow. When
the industry was visited there had been a failure of a complete crop of honesty, and only one girl and two men were
at work, but it was expected that from eighteen to twenty
employees would be needed when the industry was in full
swing again. The cultivation of honesty seems to be in an
experimental stage, little being known as yet about the soil
and climate which may be suited to it. Care is needed in
handling the branches, but the outfit required is of the
simplest description, consisting only of tables at which to
work and a stove on which to boil the dye. The curious
products of the industry are sold through agents to fancy
shops and house furnishers.

Labour in the Rural Factories

Many of the small rural factory industries were for
a long time enabled to hold their own by reason of the cheap
labour, both of indoor employees and of outworkers, which
was obtainable in the villages. Since the fixing of Trade
Board rates for certain industries has caused the same wages
to be payable in the rural districts as in London or any
industrial centre, any advantages which the remote rural
situation still retains are likely to be outweighed by its disadvantages, one of the chief of which is the high cost of
carriage, both for raw material and finished goods, over a
long distance. In those cases, however, in which the country
factories are not merely branches of a big industry in one of
the main manufacturing centres, but are themselves the
main representatives of the whole industry, there is less
labour organization and the wages paid are determined
more by local conditions.

Most of the work in these factories is done by women and girls, since the men are more fully employed on the land, or in the more characteristic *rural* industries, such as the under-wood and timber industries and basket-making. It is surprising that there seems to be, as a rule, no attempt to organize the work of the rural factory in such a way as to dovetail it in with the work on the land, and thus provide seasonal employment for those workers—many women and a few men—whose labour is only needed in agriculture during certain months of the year. The Boston pea factories, it is true, are organized on this system ; it was stated in the district that some of the factories are actually closed down from May to October when the demands for labour for potato-lifting, fruit-picking and other seasonal work are greater than can be supplied by the villages. Before the war much of this work was done by the gangs of Irishmen who came over to England for the season ; in recent years bands of the un-employed from Grantham (men who normally worked in the engineering and agricultural implement factories there), have been brought to the Fen Country for this work. But the women who work during the winter in the pea factories, or in their homes as outworkers for the factories, do a great deal of this seasonal agricultural work in the summer months. This is a case, however, of women from the towns being engaged for seasonal work on the land, and not of village women who work in the fields during the summer being employed in factories during the winter. There does not seem to be in England any rural factory organized on the system in force in Russia before the Revolution in connexion with the spirit distilleries which existed on many large estates, where the peasants who were occupied during about eight months of the year on the vast potato crops, were employed during the winter in the factory in which the spirit was distilled from the potatoes.

Some of the rural factory industries are so little adapted to their environment that they are subject to a slack season during the winter, when the workers in agriculture and the industries supplementary to it are also likely to be suffering from unemployment. This is the case in the machine-knitting industry, which seems to be particularly liable to fluctuations in trade. In one case, during a trade slump, the finishers were trained to make lingerie and blouses, the knitted garments, formerly hand-finished, being put together by machinery. This experiment, although involving con-siderable outlay, seems to have been successful and certainly

resulted in nearly all the girls being kept in employment. In
other cases, however, through lack either of enterprise or of
capital, the hours of work have been curtailed during the
winter or some of the workers dismissed. In an industry of
this kind, the plan of making on stock during the winter,
when there is little *immediate* demand for the goods, cannot
be adopted because a change of fashion may render the stock
almost worthless. The development of an alternative
occupation is a method almost as easy if the slack season
occurs periodically, and certainly safer. The peculiar
difficulty, to the workers in a rural factory, of these slack
winter periods, is that there is no alternative employment for
them, as there would more probably be in a large manufacturing town.

Some industries, such as the small glove-knitting factories
in the south of Bedfordshire and in Herts., can rely upon the
work of young girls who are well able to do the light and easy
work on the machines used ; these are set to the pattern
required and the ' carriage ' is then pushed backwards and
forwards by hand ; the seams of the gloves are stitched up on
another machine. The wages in factories of this kind are
very low, and after a few years the girls usually leave to seek
more remunerative employment elsewhere. In the machine-
knitting factories of the south-west of England, where
jumpers, coats, and other garments are made, the wages
would seem to be rather higher, both women and girls being
employed and few girls under sixteen being found at work
here. The work of the ' finishers ' here requires more skill,
and even the knitters on the machines must be more versatile
than those who only make gloves, for the designs of the garments are changed constantly in accordance with the
fashions. The payment is by piece rates, and in the winter of
1920–1 it varied from £1 to 46s. a week. In the gloving
trade it was said that the employers generally prefer to
employ girls and boys straight from school, who learn the
work quickly and do not ask high wages. Young girls,
however, are apt to be careless in working the machines
for ' fashioned ' knitting. If the manager or employer in one
of these small factories can look after the machines and keep
them in repair there may be no other man employed ; sometimes there is one mechanic, in addition to the girls and
women. In the larger firms the finishing processes are often
done to a great extent on machines, garments of a cheaper
quality being produced, but in one comparatively large
factory there were as many as seventy finishers to ninety

knitters employed ; in a smaller workroom the staff included
thirteen knitters and fourteen finishers in addition to half a
dozen packers, overseers, and other workers. In this particular industry there is no labour organization and therefore no
fixed standard of wages ; in at least one factory the wages
were very low, but on the whole the workers considered that
they were well off.

In the tooth-brush industry most of the indoor workers are
men, although some hundreds of women were employed, in
1921, as outworkers. In the collar-making industry many
women are employed, both as indoor hands and as outworkers ; married women generally prefer outwork, but in
one factory special hours were arranged for them to enable
them to get the children off to school before coming to the
factory in the morning and to return home in time to prepare
the evening meal for the family. This industry comes under
a Trade Board, and therefore the wages earned by unmarried
women and girls, who often had no dependants and no
separate household expenses, were high in comparison with
those of agricultural workers who were the chief wage-earners
of a family. In the gloving industry the earnings have also
been fixed by a Trade Board, and in 1920–1 it was said that
some of the girls working on power-driven machines could
earn as much as £3 a week, and many earned over £2 a week,
whilst the workers on treadle-machines, paid by the same
piece rates, did not earn so much. Power-driven machines
seem to be replacing those worked by foot treadles, although
it is said that the work is rather better done on the latter.

In the Wilton carpet factories the hand-weaving is done
by girls ; in one of the factories men are employed to work
the power-looms which are used here for weaving the plain
carpets. Although the hand-weavers must be fairly skilled
they are not highly paid, but the work is pleasant enough
and the varied designs and colours of the carpets make it
interesting.

Wages in the Boston pea-picking factories were said to
vary with the agricultural wages of the district, being always
slightly above these. Agricultural wages here are always on
a comparatively high level and there is a great deal of piece-
work. In December 1922 women on the land were earning
5d. an hour or from 18s. to £1 per week and men were paid
7d. an hour or 28s. 6d. a week. The factory wages for women
were at this time from 25s. to 28s. a week.

It has been said of south-country people that they are
not good workers on mechanical processes in factories

' because they have too much soul ', a state which is perhaps akin to that of those who have ' the artistic temperament '. In reviewing the small industries which have been treated in another volume [1] it was certainly found that a considerable number of these handicraft enterprises, in which there is plenty of scope for the development of individual talent, flourish in the southern counties, although there are also other parts of England, particularly the Lake District, which seem to be congenial to them. But a consideration of the craft-work of the peasantry of any district of Europe, which is still comparatively untouched by industrialism and the influences of modern urban existence, leads one to the conclusion that there is considerable skill in craftsmanship and capacity for original design latent in almost all people in that stage of civilization when the whole work of shaping the natural pro-ducts of the earth into the things they need for their daily life is still in the hands of the ordinary village craftsman. Under these conditions craftsmanship is a part of the ordinary life of the village and is imbued with a strong personal element and very closely related to local needs. In the modern factory we see the opposite state of affairs ; a workman may be engaged on one simple process ; he need not understand much of the nature of the material he works up ; he has not to consider how best it can be shaped to his own ends ; he has no care as to whence it comes (probably, so far as he is concerned, vaguely ' from abroad '), nor who will use the finished article. When he himself needs a new coat or a plate or cup he does not ask a neighbour to make it for him, but buys it in a shop without a thought as to the worker who made it.

In our village industries we still find something of the spirit of craftsmanship, in, for example, the work of the village wheelwright and in the few characteristic local industries which still survive, such as the Kingscliffe turnery. The factory workers of the towns, who have lost this spirit of craftsmanship, have, through long training, acquired new and different faculties ; the ability to perform one simple action over and over again at the greatest possible speed, to endure the monotony of this sort of work, to make their daily labour not an integral important part of their lives—their main interest and an expression of personality—but a thing to be endured, to be got through as quickly as possible.

In the small rural factories we find the transition state ;

[1] See Vol. III, *Decorative Crafts*, particularly Chap. I, ' Home Crafts and Industries '.

the village worker in a rural district may still possess some of the qualities of the craftsman although he may have been drilled into factory discipline. It is a problem whether he can only become a thoroughly efficient factory worker when all his natural ability to do individual craft work has been swamped by the acquired ability to repeat some simple action at great speed for eight hours a day ; or whether, even in a factory, this craft-skill cannot be turned to account.

Many of the small rural factories are organized on lines similar to those which govern large town factories. But in a few cases there is a definite attempt to give scope for individual work and design, and some of these attempts have met with considerable success. Even in an industry so far removed from primitive craftsmanship as machine knitting the adaptability of country workers has proved a valuable asset. It is possible that the rapid spread in the country districts of the south of England of this industry of quite recent foundation is due, to a certain extent, to the fact that country girls, unused to work in factories, have proved to be capable of skilled and original work. The manager of one workshop spoke of the ease with which the 'finishers', when turned on to blouse-making during a slack period, became skilled in the new work. In another small workshop an interesting experiment was tried. At the end of every six months the girls go in for a competition, during which they are paid according to their average piece-work earnings, whilst they produce new 'models' according to their own ideas. Each knitter consults with a finisher as to the making up of the garment and any decoration that is needed, the entries are judged by the vote of all the workers, and those models which are thought good enough are sent to the shops as samples for orders. This system promotes amongst the workers a lively interest in their work and leads to the discovery of talent and originality. It is particularly suited to an industry of this kind, the success of which depends upon the constant production of new designs.

In the tooth-brush industry there is another example of skilled work and the ability to adapt the method to the material used. The bones from which the handles and backs of the brushes are made have to be shaped by the use of a file ; owing to the varied shapes of the bones little of the shaping can be done by machinery, but the men who do this work show considerable skill.

The chip-basket factories offer the greatest contrast to the smaller workshops in which there is scope for original craftsmanship. The heavier work of cutting the chips, or thin strips of wood, from which the baskets are woven, is done by machinery. The actual weaving and finishing of the baskets is done by girls, but the work is subdivided so that each girl only performs one very simple process, passing the basket on to her neighbour for the next process.

The workers in the small rural factories are of various types, according to the kind of work which they are called upon to do. Perhaps the roughest were to be seen in the big factory of the hatters' furriers in Suffolk; the factory is filled with the noise of machinery and a nauseous smell, and the air seems to be permeated with flying hair and dust, although there is machinery for getting rid of it by means of suction. The machinery used is of the most elaborate kind, particularly that in which the skin is sliced off the pelt in the tiniest shreds, so that the fur comes out in one smooth sheet, after which it is rolled up in a bundle and packed for transport to the velour factory.

Factory work is often preferred by country girls because it has certain obvious advantages over the few alternative occupations which are open to them; they have more freedom than in domestic service, it is generally easier, less tiring, and pleasanter than laundry work, nearly always lighter than field work, and offering a better chance of regular employment. Even where wages are low, girls are glad to enter the factories. In some country districts there is, however, a prejudice against factories, and it is important that there should be good forewomen. Although married women often find outwork more convenient, the young girls and unmarried women enjoy the companionship of other workers in the factory.

Prospects of Future Development for Rural Factories

One of the greatest difficulties against which the small rural factory may have to contend is the competition with a larger—urban—factory, producing the same goods. In those industries in which both urban and rural factories are found, there is always a keen controversy about the wages which should be paid in the respective districts. The rural firms hold that a lower wage should be permissible in a country district, where the general level of wages is lower, as is also the cost of living; from the employer's point of view, also, a lower wages bill is needed to counterbalance higher cost of transport. On the other hand, urban employers will point out that the rural factory has advantages in the shape of space for expansion or for storage, more easily obtained and at lower rents. The problem is an extremely difficult one to solve ; undoubtedly the fact that outwork for factories, paid for at low rates, has existed as a possible additional means of livelihood for the farm workers' family has, in the past, helped to keep agricultural wages lower than a reasonable standard of living would require. On the other hand, where Trade Board rates have been fixed for an industry which has both urban and rural branches, these rates have often seemed to press hardly upon the rural employers. Yet if different rates were fixed for the different districts, all kinds of new difficulties might obviously arise, particularly where the districts meet or even overlap.

In the brush industry there has been very bitter feeling between the big urban firms and the small country workshops. This industry has come under a Trade Board, but the piece rates were very difficult to fix, because in some districts certain processes were done by men which, in other districts, were done by women. The fixing of the rates was said to have led to the employment of a greater number of women in the place of men, particularly in the country workshops, where much of the bristling is done by hand, but it is also leading to the introduction of machines, where possible, to replace this hand work. The brush-making industry is one which seems to be capable of being carried on successfully on the smallest scale, in the shape of a family industry, with less than half a dozen workers ; it is therefore quite likely that these small workshops with their local market will survive so long as they maintain the good quality of their work. High rates of wages affect a ' family ' industry less than any other, because even though the sons and daughters may be employed by their father as ordinary wage earners, it is possible that they, with a personal interest in the industry itself, will maintain a higher output than an ' outsider ', whether they are paid by time or by piece rates.

For rural boot factories, on the other hand, there seems to be little hope of survival, except for a few examples in remote neighbourhoods, where some particular type of boot is made for a local market. Unfortunately, a fairly widespread market is needed to absorb the output of the smallest factory which can be economically carried on. As a general rule the small boot works have already died out, unable to compete with mass production and the multiple shops.

The chip-basket industry exists chiefly in the neighbour-

hood of the strawberry growing areas. In this industry
the competition between two types of factory is to be found
only between the very small scale industry in the Cheddar
district and the much larger factories elsewhere. There does
not seem, however, to have been much direct competition,
up to the time that the Cheddar district was visited in 1920,
the small workshops here supplying most of the local
demands. There is foreign competition in this industry,
but the English manufacturers seem well able to hold
their own.

The glove industry was very prosperous during the war,
and many new firms were started, both in urban and rural
districts ; but so soon as imports began to come in again
in considerable quantities after the war, the English glove
industry, including both fabric and leather gloves, flagged ;
many of the new factories were closed down, and many
workers, particularly the outworkers, lost their employment. It is chiefly, however, as an outwork industry that
the factory gloving industry affects rural districts. The
hand-sewing of gloves by members of Women's Institutes
and other home workers not employed by factories, started
originally as a hobby, has in some cases developed into small
industries, but these are carried on along different lines
from those of any factory industry.[1]

In the case of the tooth-brush industry the possibility
of supplementary industries for the use of the waste material,
of which there is a great deal, seems to be worth considering.
Only from certain bones can the handles be cut, one manufacturer having stated that there are only ten bones in an
ox which are suitable for this purpose. The manufacturers
buy the special bones which they need from the London
soap manufacturers, but after the handles have been blocked
out there remain pieces of bone which could probably be
used for making other small articles. The workers are
skilled in carving the handles and could probably learn to
cut out other things. This industry also depends largely
upon the outworkers, who put in the bristles by hand. Bone
brushes cannot be bristled by machine, but the competition
from celluloid brushes, which can be made entirely by
machinery, is affecting the trade.

Perhaps the position of the small rural factory is best
illustrated by the machine-knitting industry, one which
has grown up in country districts in recent years, and seems
to be peculiarly fitted to be carried on in small country

[1] Vol. III, *Decorative Crafts*, Chap. I, ' Home Crafts and Industries '.

workshops. Its special characteristics have been fully described—the opportunities which it gives for original work and the value of such work, more easily produced in a small workshop, to the industry ; its markets, which, with their constant demands for new designs, keep the industry ever busy and alive. There is a school of hosiery in Leicester for the benefit of the industry, but it has been suggested that, since it has taken so firm a root in the south-western counties, the Art and Technical Schools there might provide instruction in crafts connected with the trade, such as the designing of garments. Knitted goods are cheaper than those made of woven materials, because the process is quicker and requires less elaborate machinery, and because when, as on the ' fashioned-knitting ' machines, the parts of a garment are made of the shape required and then sewn together, there is no waste of material, as there is when garments are cut out from lengths of woven stuff. Knitted garments, therefore, are likely to retain their popularity, and many developments in the industry seem possible.

The rural factory has, in some cases, grown into a replica of its town cousin, and in such cases the building of dwellings for the workers, the opening of the small shops which inevitably arise, and the development of railway facilities, may soon convert a rural into an urban area. But other types of rural factories seem likely to remain for a long time in their present form, the labour which can be drawn from a country district of a few miles in area sufficing for their needs. It is the development of these that will be of the greatest interest from the point of view of rural economics. To what extent they can widen and vary their activities without greatly increasing their size ; by what means they can fit themselves into the lives of the agricultural population, providing additional employment during the slack seasons of agriculture ; how they can take advantage of the small scale of their organization by encouraging individual and original work, at the same time keeping down the cost of production by the use of labour-saving machinery for simple processes—these are problems which have been successfully worked out in a few factories, but which are more often neglected by the rural firms. It is upon the wise solution of them that the future of the small rural factory as such must depend.

INDEX